PRAISE FOR DYNAMIC ALIGNMENT

Having recently retired from a long career in the practice of law, I found this book to be of great help in focusing my newly free time on those activities that I most truly enjoy doing.

— MARK SILVERMINTZ, RETIRED ATTORNEY

Dynamic Alignment is particularly refreshing because it doesn't try to pretend there is one magic formula for everyone. It is a joy to read about Brad and Holly's own experiences. Their authentic approach is designed to help others find fulfillment.

— N. A. ROSSI, AUTHOR

An absolutely fabulous book. My husband and I both read it. It made us think about how we can plan and implement the next stage in our lives.

— SUE QUELCH, WRITER ON TRAVEL, ENVIRONMENT & SUSTAINABILITY TOPICS

What more could you want from two guides when you are about to embark on a life affirming journey. An ultramarathon, kickboxer who likes making podcasts and an adventurer and polar traveler who likes rummaging in the wisdom of some of the greatest achievers in history and putting it into books. This is a guidebook of sorts, leading you through your journey so far and giving you the tools to plan the next stage and the stages beyond. Brad and Holly each contribute great insights which is added to by the wisdom drawn from a wide range of people that we have all heard of and who have all achieved great things.

— STELLA PARIS, AUTHOR

I loved the practical approach of *Dynamic Alignment*. It's really helpful in getting more clarity on where to direct my efforts and I've already started applying the techniques ."

— HELEN DWIGHT, MARKETING EXECUTIVE
AT LEADING HIGH TECH COMPANIES.

My aha moment with *Dynamic Alignment* was that I did some of this successfully in my professional and volunteer community journey in a more ad-hoc way. Reading this book I now can better frame up these prior success and bring new energy to upcoming goals.

— RICHARD D. BLUMBERG, PRESIDENT,
WORLD SALES SOLUTIONS, LLC AND
AUTHOR, *JOB SEEKING WARRIORS - A
MENTORS GUIDE TO WINNING!*

DYNAMIC ALIGNMENT

THE POWER OF FINDING YOUR PURPOSE,
ACHIEVING YOUR GOALS, AND LIVING A
PASSION-DRIVEN LIFE

BRAD BORKAN

HOLLY WORTON

To everyone who believed we could each achieve a few of our many goals. Thank you.
Holly and Brad

Tribal Publishing Ltd
Kemp House
124 City Road
London EC1V 2NX
UK

ISBN 978-1-911161-92-9 ebook

ISBN 978-1-911161-93-6 paperback

ISBN 978-1-911161-95-0 hardcover

ISBN 978-1-911161-94-3 workbook

CONTENTS

1

WHAT IS DYNAMIC ALIGNMENT

> "Knowing others is intelligence; knowing yourself is true wisdom."
>
> — LAO TZU

Why is it that some people wake up energized, raring to go, enthralled with all the challenges ahead? They encounter obstacles and enjoy the challenges of overcoming them. They hear the naysayers, critics (both external and internal) and all who say that what they are trying to do is not possible, not good enough, or never will be successful, and ignore the noise.

What is it that these people have in common? Can it be encapsulated into a formula that anyone can use today?

These questions and ones like them kept coming back to us. We are authors and friends, and have both puzzled over this—for a very long time individually, and more recently collectively—thinking about questions like these and seeking the answers.

Holly created over 500 podcasts in her *Into the Woods with Holly Worton* podcast series on topics related to motivation, goals, achievement and setbacks, during which she interviewed hundreds of people. Brad has written books about great achievers of the past 200 years such as the early Antarctic explorers like Ernest Shackleton and Roald Amundsen as well as others like Theodore Roosevelt, who was instrumental in building the Panama Canal, the Wright Brothers, and Susan B. Anthony and Elizabeth Cady Stanton—two American women who pioneered the women's rights movement in the 1800s.

When we put our collective knowledge and experiences together, what emerged was not just that such a phenomenon exists in some people, but that what they are doing to be energized and raring to go, can be encapsulated in an 8-step process.

We gave it the name *Dynamic Alignment*. This book explains our process.

Why Dynamic Alignment is different

Our approach differs from other approaches in self-help books and strategies.

It's not about "correcting" things that you are doing wrong, nor is it about fixing perceived weaknesses in you or your lifestyle. It's not a set of detailed exercises (though we do provide a workbook for those who like that sort of thing). This book can be read from cover to cover in an hour or two. The approach entails a mindset shift that you can blend into everything else that you are doing. You can adopt all of it or some elements of it into your own philosophies and style of working and being. You can come back to it time and again.

Nothing in our process is rigid. It is not prescriptive. We don't say you have to do it only our way. Our aim is that it be flexible to match you, your personality, how you see the world, and how you like to do things.

Dynamic Alignment can give you a fresh perspective on

yourself and your life's journey. The process emphasizes the dynamic, changing, evolving nature of life and work, encouraging you to continually refine and update what you are doing and how you are thinking about what you are doing.

It enables you to make small or big pivots as you evolve. A Dynamically Aligned life becomes an ongoing and thrilling experience, where self-awareness and finding your multi-passionate life work in tandem with your own goals, aspirations and desires. Together all of this creates a more invigorating and fulfilling life.

The benefits of this become evident as you gain clarity on what thrills you, and discover ways to enhance your strengths, and attract people, resources and opportunities into your life to help you along the way.

An overview of the process

The first step is a concept called the Life Factor Building Blocks (LFBB), which help you to understand yourself better. The aim of the LFBBs is to help you identify, understand, and appreciate *all* of the talents, values, and experiences (both the good ones and the bad ones) that combined create the unique "you"—the person you are today.

Dynamic Alignment is not about changing you. It's about embracing your uniqueness, and rejoicing in your value and insights from a life well-experienced. It's about appreciating the specialness of your character and how it was shaped by various events, people and circumstances.

Step 2 is to look at the things you love doing—not just now, but throughout your life. You'll look at your interests, hobbies and work over the years, and understand how your pastimes and passions have evolved. This results in a list called your UIS —your Unique Interest Set.

Once you have identified your UIS, Step 3 is about looking

at all the different ways you can combine elements of your various interests to create different and unique paths and actions—ones that are uniquely yours, that only you can deliver. Even if you don't pursue any of these, this part of the process opens you up to new perspectives and opportunities.

Then, Step 4 involves dabbling, which is a term we adopted for trying out specific combinations of your interests to explore what excites and energizes you and even has the potential to be monetized. Once you actually start dabbling, you may find that you don't want to pursue certain paths or you want to pursue different paths. You don't have to monetize all your interests; some can remain as hobbies or just remain dormant. It's not about creating a side-hustle. It's about creating something that you can uniquely do—that absolutely thrills you—because of who you are.

Step 5 has to do with goals based on combinations of elements in your UIS, but our approach to goals is different from other styles of goal-setting that say you have to set goals and then strive to achieve them. We encourage you to think about your goal language—what types of goals motivate you most? You may set easy, simple or detailed goals, stretch goals or no goals—it's up to you, based on your own goal language and what motivates you. As you will see, there are many different goal styles. The key is finding yours.

Step 6 involves working towards your goals. In the previous step, you may have set easily attainable milestone goals or harder ones. Whatever style you choose, determining chunk-size intermediary desires that fit your own goal language can help you get there.

As you undertake this journey, we think something will happen. You will start attracting people, resources, opportunities, connections, and possibilities into your life—all of which can help you achieve your UIS. We call this Life Magnetism.

Step 7 is about spotting when Life Magnetism is happening and using it to propel you forward.

The final part of the Dynamic Alignment process, Step 8, occurs as your life continues and evolves. There will be opportunities to dynamically refine, update, and align your Life Factor Building Blocks, UIS, combinations of elements from your UIS, and goals to make little or big adjustments to propel you further.

All these steps combine to make life a more thrilling experiment.

Will Dynamic Alignment help you?

Will this 8-step Dynamic Alignment process help you? That depends on many factors.

The approach is designed to be thought-provoking, and the information you glean about yourself and your interests could serve you for the rest of your life.

It *might* encourage you to think differently about your experiences, skills, talents, and desires. It *might* open your understanding of your uniqueness and how to use that uniqueness to your advantage. It *might* reveal new ways to monetize some of your skills.

We hope it will be entertaining.

And energizing.

Before we get started, we'd like to take a few minutes to explain how we discovered Dynamic Alignment.

2

HOW WE DISCOVERED DYNAMIC ALIGNMENT

"Know what sparks the light in you. Then use that light to illuminate the world."

— *OPRAH WINFREY*

In the conversations that led to this book, what we noticed was that we each had a variety of interests that to the other person seemed almost random. The question we found ourselves asking was: why would you have those interests? As a collection, if you wrote them down on paper, they seemed unconnected.

Holly described her interests from a young age as reading, writing, and ... no, not arithmetic: the third one was plants. Brad's were Antarctica, wondering why people make the decisions they do, and technology.

Neither of us could fully comprehend each other's list because each of our interests were so far removed from the other's point of view. We found that we were curious about the reasons for each person's choice of interests because to the other person, not only did what they were interested in seem disconnected from the person's other interests, they also seemed almost randomly chosen.

What we came to realize was what a person likes, or what their interests are, were not judgment issues. A person likes what they like for a variety of reasons.

We talked about other things that interested us. As Holly grew older, her list expanded to include Spanish and travel. She had lived for several years in Spain and various Latin American countries. Later in her life, her interests expanded into hiking, camping, and sports like kickboxing and running ultramarathons.

Brad's list was different and not as extensive. He became more interested in the achievements of great people doing science, exploring the polar regions, and people and small teams who undertook monumental endeavors. His focus was, "What is it that drives epic achievement in some people?"

What we were learning from this was:

1. We needed to stop being judgmental about the other person's interests. Just because they are not our interests, doesn't make them wrong, bad or incongruent.
2. Our core interests came about from high school days or even earlier but changed and evolved over time, influenced by our experiences and other factors.

There was something else that was becoming evident. To the other person, the interests seemed a hodgepodge. To the owner of those interests, they seemed totally rational.

The explanations we discovered were that we each had factors that drove us and motivated us—internally or externally—even if it was simply to prove to ourselves that we could do it, such as Holly's running in ultramarathons or Brad's living on a ship for a month in the roughest seas in the world in the

Southern Ocean. It didn't matter if we were doing this for internal "prove I can do it" purposes, for "look at me" purposes, or for research purposes—or some combination of those. What was key was it was a personal interest.

Because it is there

It didn't matter that Holly was a non-sporty person in high school and university. She was able to develop intense sports interests later in life and pursue them. It also didn't matter that Brad hates being cold, is prone to seasickness on even the gentlest bays and rivers, and dislikes being on ships. Each person's drive to do what they wanted to do was strong—strong enough to overcome all other factors.

We started wondering, "Why was that?"

The answer we came up with was the same as what the acclaimed British mountaineer George Mallory said in 1922 when he was asked by a journalist, "Why would you want to climb Everest?" His reply was simply, "Because it is there."

The answer to why Holly might want to enter an ultramarathon is her own choice. The drive and motivation for doing so are also her own, even if it comes down to "Because it is there." What was most interesting was discovering the energizing strength of that desire.

We started assessing this in relation to our own work. Using Holly's podcast interviews and Brad's analysis of historical people who achieved at extraordinary levels, what we concluded was:

If a person can really tap into what motivates them at a deeply personal and innate level, there is not much that will stop them from striving for it.

This was as true for the Victorian engineer Isambard

Kingdom Brunel who designed and built great bridges, tunnels, and railways across Britain in the 1800s as it was for the Wright brothers in the early 1900s trying to invent the airplane, or for people living today who aren't striving to work at these epic levels, but seeking a meaningful and energized life.

The key is the collection of activities

The challenge was: How do you find this? We gave this more thought, again going back to our source material—Holly's podcasts and Brad's books.

What we discovered was that while any activity could be motivating in itself, what was truly motivating was the *collection of activities* that the person was interested in.

To put this another way, it wasn't the individual actions that were motivating. It was:

> *The* **combined set of pursuits** *a person was pursuing that became both self-fulfilling and motivational.*

Pursuing one activity would not in and of itself be motivational enough to overcome obstacles for most people. It had to do with the combined pursuits. This combination, which resonated uniquely for the person involved, reinforced their achievement-driven behavior. This in turn drove the individual activities to achieve the end goal.

For polar explorers like Ernest Shackleton or Roald Amundsen it was the combination of pursuits and drivers that motivated them—achieving glory in Antarctica was driven not just by being first, but for the acclaim for their nation and king, for science and discovery, and for personal recognition and fame.

There had to be multiple drivers *and* multiple passions

being aroused at the same time. All of those worked together to create within a person an unstoppable drive.

What we realized was this: all of these needed to be directly connected to what it is that makes a specific person tick.

But there is more

We further realized that there needed to be added synergy from the confluence of activities that the person was engaged in.

For example, once Holly became proficient at kickboxing, she started setting goals like achieving the next level of certification, ultimately leading to her earning her black belt. Holly also goes on long, multi-day solo hikes which are a source of content for the books she has written on trekking, nature, and hiking paths.

Since there's an element of risk in being a solo walker, her black belt in kickboxing gives her added confidence in defending herself should the need arise. And all of this gave her added content for her podcast.

So, there was a combination of activities that worked together to create one overarching strong motivational drive. Obstacles such as being too tired to train melted away in the face of this drive.

We noticed this in other people's pursuits as well. The combination of interests may have seemed unusual to an outside observer until seen from the doer's perspective. Then we could see the motivating power of a collection of interests.

The key was not seeing multiple different interests such as kickboxing as one interest, hiking as another interest, and writing books about hikes as a third interest, but seeing them as one, single, deeply motivating *collection of interests* with multiple components.

Ultimately, the true energizing power comes when each of these components becomes a deep passion and the overarching desire becomes connected to the life factors, beliefs and experiences of that individual.

Combinations of interests leads to Life Magnetism

Back in 2021, Holly had a dream of running an ultramarathon, even though she wasn't sure it was possible for her. She had another goal: to achieve her black belt in kickboxing. While each goal was motivational, the real power that she was discovering was in combining them. Here's why: the two reinforced one another, creating a synergy. The stamina to train for and run an ultramarathon was helping her with kickboxing, and the fitness training for kickboxing was helping her ultramarathon preparation.

What Holly was finding was this:

If one goal was motivating, two or more goals each relevant to her specific interests were exponentially motivating, especially when the combined pursuits *had a mutual benefit for each and all of her activities.*

Brad was finding similar results. One goal was to write his next book, and while doing so, another goal was to write a magazine article for a leading business publication. A third goal was to appear on a major leadership podcast show, and a fourth goal was to be more active in the Antarctic community such as attaining a place on the committee of the Friends of the Scott Polar Research Institute.

What he was finding was the multiple goals worked together to be more motivating. The book brought recognition, which led to writing magazine articles. Speaking on podcast shows helped him hone the way he described the lessons from the early Antarctic explorers. All of this opened doors to meet people at the Scott Polar Research Institute.

It was in discussing these stories that we realized something startling:

When pursuing these multiple goals, a magnetism was happening. The more the goals were being pursued, the more doors started opening.

It was like a snowball effect: the more these goals, which were unique to Holly or Brad, were pursued, the more *resources, support, help, and people* were being attracted to make them a reality.

For example, having a desire to write an article for a leading business publication is a far cry from actually doing so. Desiring to be interviewed on a top leadership podcast series is a long shot for a relatively unknown person. These are things that need to be worked up to by writing for lesser publications or appearing on unknown or little-known podcast shows—or by having someone in your network who can help you get these types of opportunities.

Fortunately, "A journey of a thousand miles begins with a single step." This common saying from a Chinese proverb is how it works with achieving big goals. Learning to trek on long, strenuous trails or successfully completing ultramarathon races is a journey that starts with gentler and shorter trails and races. The journey to a black belt starts with a white belt and moves through all the colors in which belts are available. Each small activity opened another door, created another contact, or revealed an opportunity that wouldn't have otherwise been spotted or offered if Holly had been approaching it haphazardly.

Her goal-focused mindset attracted opportunities, people and resources that would not have otherwise been available— and had they been available earlier, they might not have been recognized for what they were.

What surprised us in our conversations was that Brad experienced the same phenomenon. Writing blogs and articles on

LinkedIn led to writing a few guest blogs on other people's websites, and being invited to be interviewed on some podcast shows, some of which may only have had a few people who listened to them. Each endeavor opened another door which led to another collaboration, a podcast interview or a writing or speaking opportunity.

It might be easy to dismiss this as luck or simply say, "Well, of course, this is the law of *starting small*," but what we each discovered independently was that starting small was only part of it. It was that we were each pursuing a collection of endeavors *unique* to us, which in itself was energizing to us, and then became even more energizing because opportunities, resources and people who could help or could open doors were being attracted to our pursuits.

And we discovered that it wasn't just us.

Other people told us that when they were involved in multiple combined pursuits they had experienced similar effects. We called this phenomenon Life Magnetism.

All of this came together in a way that enabled us to define the Dynamic Alignment 8-step process.

In the next chapters, we explain the 8 steps and show you how to achieve Dynamic Alignment in your own life. Step 1 has to do with Life Factor Building Blocks.

3

STEP 1: LIFE FACTOR BUILDING BLOCKS

"Knowing yourself is the beginning of all wisdom."

— *ARISTOTLE*

The first step in gaining Dynamic Alignment is understanding and appreciating all that makes you, "you." What makes you unique? This can be done with a simple technique that we devised.

We call it the **Life Factor Building Blocks**. All experiences —good and bad, successful or unsuccessful—shape your attitudes and your view of the world.

These experiences help to define what you enjoy doing and what you find unpleasant. Studying and analyzing your Life Factor Building Blocks can help you determine your UIS — Unique Interest Set.

Below is our list of Life Factor Building Blocks (LFBB). It's quite extensive. There are likely items you can add and perhaps some you want to remove or recategorize. Some items are listed in more than one category.

How you interpret, classify and experience all these

factors determines your personality and outlook on life. It's worth scanning through the list and identifying some in each category to think about. We've provided a few sample questions to aid your thinking. These are optional. The key to this step is thinking about some of the various elements in each category.

The totality of the Life Factor Building Blocks is proof that each human being is truly unique. Many people can have the same profession, be born in the same year, grow up in the same town, or even be in the same family, yet each person is totally unique because of their own experiences—and how they interpret those experiences.

The Categories

We divided the building blocks into 14 categories.

1. Actions
2. Aspirations
3. Learning Experiences
4. Life Challenges
5. Life Experiences
6. Life Successes
7. Money
8. People in Your Life
9. Perspectives/ Attitudes
10. Preferences
11. Propensities
12. Relationships
13. Where You Live
14. Work Experiences

Each category is important, and it's not for us to determine the priority. It is up to you, as the order of priority will be unique to each individual. For this reason, the categories are listed in alphabetical order.

The elements within each of these categories are listed (again in alphabetical order, so you can determine their order of importance) and explained below.

The Life Factor Building Blocks

ACTIONS:

Actions shape who we are as individuals (so do many elements listed in other LFBB categories). People's actions and inactions reveal values, beliefs, and priorities. We do things because we want to, or deem we have to. We avoid things we don't like.

- Adventures
- Building things
- Creative projects
- Decisions you've made
- Habits
- Hobbies
- Jobs
- Leadership
- Living in other countries
- Regrets
- Risk-taking
- Socializing
- Social media engagement
- Teamwork
- Times you pursued something
- Travel

Each action we take, no matter how small, impacts our

character and personality and contributes to our overall identity. We are sure you can identify other actions, though you may find that we grouped those into other LFBB categories.

Questions to ponder:

- What are the biggest or best adventures you've had throughout your life?
- What were some of the best decisions you've made in your life?
- When have you chosen to take risks in your life?
- When have you felt successful in life? What are your biggest successes?

ASPIRATIONS:

Aspirations shape our vision of an ideal future. Pursuing aspirations also forces us to grow, learn, and develop new skills. These include:

- Desires
- Dreams
- Goals
- Intentions
- Jobs and career ambitions
- Relationships

Questions to consider:

- What have been your most important desires in life?
- If you could have any job in the world, what would it be?

LEARNING EXPERIENCES:

There are two types of learning experiences: structured learning experiences and the School of Hard Knocks. They can expand our knowledge, skills, and perspectives, and help us become more resilient and capable individuals.

- Adult education
- Apprenticeships
- Conferences, webinars and workshops
- Degrees
- Extra-curricular activities
- High school experiences
- Inspiring teachers
- Internships
- Online courses
- Pre-school and primary school experiences
- Report cards
- University experiences

Questions to consider:

- Who were your most inspiring teachers, and what did you learn from them?
- Have you continued your education in any way as an adult? How has that enriched your life?
- Have you taken any online courses that you found useful?

LIFE CHALLENGES:

Every challenge is an experience that helps mold or shape our individual character. These include:

- Being in the wrong place at the wrong time
- Break-ups of friendships or relationships
- Disappointments
- Embarrassing moments
- Failures
- Health incidents
- Obstacles
- Opportunities missed
- Unrequited love

Questions to consider:

- Did you ever come across any obstacles that you were unable to overcome? What did you do instead?
- Have you ever experienced missed opportunities? What did you learn from those experiences?
- How have the disappointments you've experienced shape your life?

LIFE EXPERIENCES:

There are so many life experiences - some big and some small, some wonderful and enriching and others not so much - that all combine to make us unique. Examples include:

- Books you've read
- Childhood and upbringing
- Family and living situations
- Moments of joy
- Moments of wonder
- Parents' relationship to one another
- Sexual experiences
- Travel experiences
- Trips and vacations

- Weddings, divorces and separations

Questions:

- Which of the books you've read has had the biggest impact on your life?
- What are the biggest moments of joy you've experienced in life? How have they affected you?
- What trips and vacations have impacted you the most?

LIFE SUCCESSES:

From a very young age there may have been moments where success is recognized internally or externally. When things work out these include:

- Academic success
- Awards
- Being in the right place at the right time
- Birthdays
- Celebrations
- Challenging situations you turned around to your advantage
- Good luck
- New friends
- Obstacles you've overcome
- Opportunities spotted
- Opportunities taken
- Problems you've solved
- Recognition of achievement
- Sporting triumphs
- Wins

Questions:

- What does success mean to you?
- Have you ever been in a challenging situation that you were able to turn around to your advantage? What did you learn from that?
- What opportunities have you taken? How did they impact your life?
- What are the biggest successes you've experienced in life?

MONEY:

Just about everyone has a challenging relationship with money. All of this helps to define our attitudes and beliefs.

- Buying profile—buying more or less than you need
- Charitable giving
- Family attitudes to money when you were growing up
- Philosophy and money mindset
- Risk profile
- Scarcity or abundance mindset
- Spender or saver

Questions:

- What's your money philosophy or money mindset?
- Do you have a sense of abundance or a sense of financial insecurity? How has that impacted your life decisions?
- Are you a spender or a saver?

PEOPLE IN YOUR LIFE:

Throughout our lives, we cross paths with thousands of people, all of whom influence us, including:

- Colleagues
- Family
- Fictional characters who inspire you
- Friends and friends of friends
- Hero figures
- Inspiring People
- Mentors
- Parents
- People who encouraged or supported you
- People who gave you comfort when needed
- People you helped
- Role models
- Social media contacts
- Strangers who became friends

Questions:

- Who are the most inspiring people in your life, and why?
- Who are the people you admire most? Why?
- Are there any significant strangers who later became friends? How did those relationships affect you?

PERSPECTIVES/ATTITUDES:

Our attitudes and perspectives form a lens through which we view our experiences. These include:

- Beliefs

- Definition of fun
- Emotions
- Glass half-full/glass half-empty
- How you cope with setbacks and obstacles
- How you process information
- Imagination
- Love
- Prejudices
- Sense of excitement
- Sense of fear
- Sense of humor
- Sense of right and wrong
- Sense of wonder
- Spirituality
- Things you've learned
- Tolerance of other people's differences
- What makes you happy or joyful
- World view

Questions:

- What things in life give you a sense of excitement?
- What things inspire a sense of wonder in you?
- What makes you happy or joyful?

PREFERENCES (Likes and dislikes):

Our likes, dislikes, and preferences form a big part of our uniqueness. These include how we feel about:

- Art
- Books
- Causes you support
- Dance

- Diversity
- Fashion
- Foods
- Lifestyle
- Literature
- Music
- Museums
- Politics
- Style
- Taste
- Theatre
- What inspires you

Questions:

- Who are your favorite musicians or composers?
- What's your personal sense of style like?
- What makes you happy in life?

PROPENSITIES (What you are born with or can develop)

We are each born with a set of elements that influence our uniqueness. Whether you call them traits, characteristics, tendencies, attributes, or propensities, these elements make up a big part of our uniqueness. Propensities include:

- Ability to make friends
- Ability to tell stories
- Ability to tolerate discomfort
- Ability to step out of your comfort zone
- Ability to tolerate unexpected situations
- Artistic and musical ability
- Can-do attitude
- Collaborative style

- Communication style
- Competitive style
- Creative ability
- Curiosity
- How you learn
- Inquisitiveness
- Joie de vivre
- Mental agility
- Open-mindedness
- Physical strengths
- Sense of humor
- Sensory focus - whether you are a visual, auditory, or kinesthetic person
- Seriousness
- Tolerance of other people
- Work ethic

Questions:

- Is it easy for you to step out of your comfort zone, or do you find it challenging?
- Are you a good storyteller, or do you struggle with it?
- What's your creative process like?

RELATIONSHIPS:

Our ability to make, nurture and value relationships with other people is an important factor in what makes us unique. This extends from our parents and family upbringing to the myriad of people we meet throughout our lives:

- Ability to welcome new people into your life
- Best friends

- Children
- Extended Family
- First love
- Girlfriends/ boyfriends
- In-laws
- Long-term and short-term friends
- Neighbors
- Parents
- Pets
- Roommates
- Siblings
- Social network
- Spouse or partner
- Teachers and professors
- Work colleagues

Questions:

- How easily do you welcome new people into your life?
- Who have been your most significant friends throughout life? How did they shape who you are?
- How have teachers or professors influenced you?

WHERE YOU LIVE

Where we live is an important part of who we are. Elements include places we grew up and the places we choose to live as adults, including:

- Community
- Continent
- Country or nation
- Home

- Houses and apartments you've lived in
- Neighborhood
- Street
- Your environment
- Your possessions

Questions

- What are the different houses and apartments you've lived in? How have they impacted you?
- What's the environment like where you live?
- What are your most prized possessions?

WORK EXPERIENCES

Every aspect of our work influences us. Elements include:

- Career and jobs
- Charity work
- Colleagues
- Employers
- Internships
- Jobs you wish you had
- Overtime work
- Pay
- Promotions
- Self-employment and entrepreneurship
- Side hustles
- Volunteer jobs, work and projects

Questions

- Who have been the most influential bosses in your life?

- Who are your most significant colleagues in your career? How have they affected you and your career?
- What have been the most significant part-time and full-time jobs in your life?

Using the Life Factor Building Blocks

By reading through these lists of building blocks and thinking about how they apply to you, it hopefully becomes clear that no one else has the exact same reaction to all of these elements and questions as you will. Each person is unique, and their character is formed by the characteristics they were born with and the experiences they had throughout their life.

Your parents cannot read through the Life Factor Building Blocks and identify how you will react to each and every one of them. Nor can your siblings or your best friend.

Your reactions to them and interpretations of them are unique. It is that uniqueness that Dynamic Alignment wants to tap into and bring out to the open to help you identify your Unique Interest Set.

Before we do that, there's an important point to address. Are there some people who read through that list and have the perfect life? The quick answer is no. In the next chapter, we explain this further and provide examples.

4

BUT DON'T SOME PEOPLE HAVE IT EASY?

" *"Life is made up of a few moments all strung together like pearls. Each moment is a pearl, and it is up to us to pick the ones with the highest luster."*

— *JOYCE HILFER*

The Life Factor Building Blocks, when taken together, make up the person you are today. You can be uniquely defined by them.

When you tackle any endeavor—big or small—how you approach it will be defined by these factors. You bring to any undertaking, opportunity, relationship or challenge a perspective uniquely shaped by these factors.

When you think this way, you are no longer defined by your profession, income, house, car, spouse, relationships or anything else. You are defined by your experiences, activities and perceptions, and the many other factors that define who you are.

This is empowering because one of the keys to feeling energized is tapping into all that makes you unique: the good and the not-so-good. Embracing and celebrating all the experiences and traits that make you unique helps define what you can uniquely contribute to the world.

And then, put them to the best use possible, which we will show you how to do in later Dynamic Alignment steps.

But don't some people have it easy?

It might be easy or even satisfying to look at successful people and think they had it lucky, or they lead a life (or led a life) without worry or setbacks. In Brad's books about the decisions made by the early Antarctic explorers like Robert Scott, Ernest Shackleton and Roald Amundsen and other people who achieved at an epic level—like the world's greatest engineer, the Victorian-era Isambard Kingdom Brunel; the cowboy turned president, Theodore Roosevelt; and others like the Wright Brothers—it is clear that each encountered their fair share of challenges.

A good example is Teddy Roosevelt. Born into one of the wealthiest American families, it is easy to envision he must have had a perfect life. His father was one of the founders of the American Museum of Natural History in New York City, and since young Theodore had a keen interest in animals and habitats, this sounds as though this must have made for an ideal life. While it was at one level, he was also small for his age, with bad asthma. Theodore Roosevelt was bullied in school and several times nearly died from asthma attacks.

He overcame his asthma by building strength through vigorous exercise. He went to Harvard, got married, and then on Valentine's Day 1884 his wife died giving birth (though their baby, Alice, lived) and on the *exact same day*, his beloved, ailing mother died. Roosevelt, at the age of 26, wrote in his diary that the light had gone out of his life.

Awful as these experiences were, they shaped him—and he

was able to find strength and determination from them years later. He was able to use his character traits, personality and experiences to shape a meaningful and consequential life. He was instrumental in the building of the Panama Canal and the formation of the US national parks.

Ernest Shackleton was a famous explorer of great acclaim, yet he never achieved the primary goal of any of his Antarctic expeditions. He was never successful in business or politics, but in recent years he has been seen as the model of great leadership.

Isambard Kingdom Brunel, who built tunnels, railways, bridges and ships, was nearly killed when the Thames Tunnel (the first tunnel ever to be built under a flowing river) that he was a lead engineer on flooded. On another occasion, during the Great Western Railway project which he designed, a locomotive toppled over after a lifting apparatus broke. He had to run for his life. Overcoming these life-endangering setbacks was part of what made him successful.

While playing ice hockey during his high school years, Wilbur Wright was struck in the face with a hockey stick and lost most of his front teeth. This was a disturbing injury that turned him into a recluse for three years, during which he shunned society and cared for his mother, who was dying of TB. During this time, he decided not to attend Yale and never went to university. He did however, along with his brother Orville, invent the airplane.

Here are other examples featuring other, less famous, people.

Doug Noll was a guest on Holly's podcast. Doug is a whitewater guide, Level III PSIA ski instructor, sailor, and fly fisher. He has also been a rock climber, mountaineer, competitive swimmer, and Class IV kayaker. It might seem like Doug is a natural-born athlete, but nothing could be further from the truth.

His achievements were made in the face of serious challenges. Doug was born with multiple disabilities: both hearing and vision disabilities as well as two club feet. After struggling with sports in school, he turned to Scouts and the outdoors and started to thrive. His various outdoor adventures taught him discipline, persistence, patience, mental endurance, and fortitude, which he applied in his career as a peacemaker and mediator. Doug now trains life inmates locked in maximum-security prisons to be peacemakers and mediators.

Tori Joy Geiger, another guest on Holly's show, is a congenital heart defect survivor and has undergone multiple open-heart surgeries and procedures throughout her life. Despite this, she was an avid athlete, participating in volleyball, basketball, and track in high school. She went on to play volleyball at Corban University and later joined the track team at George Fox University as a high jumper.

Wanting to help others affected by chronic illnesses such as congenital heart disease, Tori started a lifestyle blog where she shares lifestyle and chronic illness tips. Her mission is to help other chronic illness warriors achieve a life of fulfillment.

Walker Brandt has appeared in international blockbuster films, TV shows, and thousands of advertising campaigns and commercials for global brands. Her story, as told on Holly's podcast, is another example of someone who looks incredibly successful on paper, but in real life overcame significant adversity.

After a suicide attempt at the age of 14, Walker refused to be broken and began her independent journey to overcome the trauma of growing up in a violent alcoholic family. A voice one day told her to "Stop. Leave." Remarkably, she listened, left home as a teen runaway, and later became an emancipated minor at the age of 16. Now she tells her life story to help others to overcome similar situations.

No one has an easy journey

No one has an easy journey. All of our traits, experiences, propensities, relationships and actions determine our uniqueness. It is then up to each of us to use them, the positive ones—and even the negative ones—to propel our lives forward.

Step 2 involves taking what you gleaned as the insights from the Life Factor Building Blocks and using them to create your Unique Interest Set.

We explain how to do this in the next chapter.

5

STEP 2: CREATING YOUR UNIQUE INTEREST SET

"Be yourself; everyone else is already taken."

— *OSCAR WILDE*

Step 2 in Dynamic Alignment is listing what interests you —defining your UIS, or your Unique Interest Set.

At first glance, this can seem easy. Top-level interests could stem from your career or job and your primary hobbies. They might include what you like to read about, what you do or would like to be doing in your spare time, where you like to visit, and what occupies your thoughts. Our goal in this chapter is to help you think more broadly than you might otherwise do when creating your UIS.

The aim is that you come up with 5 to 10 items—each of which absolutely thrills you when you see the item written down. The reaction to each will hopefully be, "Yes, I absolutely love doing this" or "I *would* absolutely love doing that" or a similar reaction.

Your UIS can be a mixture of things—some nouns, some

place names, and some actions, some activities. Don't stress about the wording. Any phrases or sentences you want to use are fine. As with every step in Dynamic Alignment, the key is to make it yours—whatever style and wording works for you is fine. The only thing we suggest is you write it down, but where you write it is your choice—on paper, in a notes app, in Word or Pages or anywhere you can refer to it again and edit it or adjust it easily.

You might want to think of it as the things you most enjoy being, doing, and having. There's no right and wrong. Don't think about what other people might think about your list. It's *your* list, not theirs. Focus on your own interests, not what someone wants you to be, or what you think others want for you.

Some people might write their UIS list quickly; others might take days or weeks to think about what their interests are and tweak the list.

Please remember that your UIS is not fixed in stone. It's not a one-and-done endeavor. The whole point is it changes and evolves as you do, and as you have new life experiences those experiences will shape you even further.

There's something to consider when creating your UIS and that is what happens in Step 3, which is described in the next chapter, but we need to give you a hint here.

The Dynamic Alignment approach in defining your UIS is to go further. As you find out in Step 3, the key is *not in the individual items* in your UIS, but in the mixing and matching of the items in it, and in the synergy created by their sum total.

This is where the magic happens. It is the *combination* of <u>you</u> and <u>all the unique things that define you</u> from your Life

Factor Building Blocks—and some or all of your UIS—that result in a powerful, unstoppable, energizing combination:

YOU

+

YOUR LIFE FACTOR BUILDING BLOCKS

+

A MIX FROM YOUR UNIQUE INTEREST SET

=

YOUR *UNIQUE* CONTRIBUTION TO THE WORLD

We will explain this further in future chapters. Right now, let's focus on your UIS.

Brainstorming across four timescales

When defining your UIS, it's important to consider that there are four time scales to think about: three lifetime timescales and one that goes beyond your lifetime (your legacy) to keep in mind.

1. The Past:

Forget about what you are doing right now to earn a living and focus on your past experiences. List all the things that gave you energy, regardless of whether any of them could generate an income.

What interested you in your younger days? In later life, we often get so caught up in earning a living that it is easy to lose track of what excited us in our early days. Said another way, "When you were young, what did you want to be when you grew up?"

2. The Present:

Focusing on your life as it is today, including your job, career and lifestyle, list only the items that you *really* enjoy. Don't spend too much time deciding how to word them or even wondering if they can generate an income.

What are you doing now—this week, this month, this year —that thrills you, even if it is just fleeting? Here you can also include the recent past, such as last week or last month. Was there anything that was absolutely wonderful that you did or wish you could have done?

3. The Future:

Ignoring what's plausible, and also which areas you have talent in, if you could do anything in the future that would absolutely thrill or energize you, what would it be? What would you do if money weren't an issue and all of your needs were met?

What are things that you wish you had an interest in? This might include skills that you wish you had, perhaps artistic or acting skills. What are things you know you have an interest in but have no available time to pursue right now?

4. Your Legacy:

Ten, twenty or even fifty years after you have lived - when your relatives and others are discussing having known you or having learned about you from others, what is it that you'd want them to be saying? What would you want to be remembered for?

Creating your UIS

Creating your UIS involves taking everything from your LFBB and all that you've been thinking about from the above timescales and distilling them into things that truly energize you.

One way to think of your UIS is that it is a simple table you are filling in, like the one shown below. Add as many rows as you want. There's no maximum. We'd recommend a minimum of four items.

	Your Interests
1	
2	
3	
4	

Focus on your list and re-shape it and re-order it. Try using different words to explain your items. Which combination of item order and descriptions best provides a thrill to you?

The more you re-work and edit the list, or even scrap it and start again, the closer you will get to your Unique Interest Set.

Remember:

The list doesn't need to make sense to anyone else. The key is that it is your Unique Interest Set, not your spouse's, not your parents' or anyone else's.

In the next chapter, we will reveal how your Unique Interest Set can help you become more energized about all aspects of your life. In the meantime, let's take a look at some example UIS lists. For data protection reasons, we cannot share anyone else's so we decided to share our own. We have combined these with a bit of—hopefully not too cringeworthy, but brutally honest—personal details as to how we each derived our UIS.

Examples: Here is a brief look at the authors' UISs

Holly's UIS

Hi. Holly here! If you had told me back when I was in high school that I'd be where I am today, it probably would have sounded like fiction. In those days, I didn't have a vision for my life. I had interests and passions, but I didn't have any concept of how I could live a life that combined some or all of them.

That's why it was so difficult for me to decide what to major in when I went to university. Should I be an English major or a Journalism major, or should I major in Ornamental Horticulture? I loved reading, writing, and plants—but I had no idea how to combine the three.

Life had its twists and turns. I went off to study abroad in Spain—an adventure which satisfied my passion for the Spanish language and sparked a new passion for travel, then I taught English in Costa Rica, and eventually I ended up studying abroad again during grad school, this time in Mexico. A list of my past interests would have been:

	Holly's Interests
1	Reading
2	Writing
3	Nature: plants and trees
4	Spanish
5	Travel

After a few more detours, I began my first business in Mexico, in the hospitality industry. With a business partner, I co-owned three ecohotels. From there, we expanded the company into Argentina and Chile.

Sounds glamorous and successful, doesn't it? It was neither.

I had no idea how to run a business, and I had never before worked in hospitality. This was an incredibly challenging time of my life. I managed the hotel, the restaurant and bar, and also handled room reservations and online marketing for the business.

Eventually, I said goodbye to this endeavor. While living in Argentina, I took a year-and-a-half-long sabbatical to figure out what I wanted to do next. I spent the time cooking, knitting, going to the gym, painting, and blogging.

Cooking was something that I had never really enjoyed, but since I had lots of time on my hands, I began to delight in experimenting with new recipes and blogging about them. Knitting was something I had always wanted to learn, and I started taking classes at a local yarn shop. I eventually learned that, while I enjoyed the meditative aspect of knitting scarves, this did not apply to bigger projects where I actually had to think about what I was doing. I was a big fan of going to the gym even before my sabbatical, and that continued. I had started my first blog a couple of years prior, in 2006, and I documented my dabbling in all these activities—as well as my general thoughts on life.

When I still had no idea what to do, I moved to England. There, I trained as a coach and set up a business helping authors use social media to connect with their readers and sell more books.

This business expanded into providing full publishing services for writers who wanted to become indie publishers. I now, along with my husband, help people to write their books and publish them—and translate them into Spanish if needed. I've been an avid blogger since 2006, and since 2013 have produced 500 podcast episodes. My present interests include:

	Holly's Additional Interests
6	Helping authors
7	Writing blogs
8	Podcasting
9	Mindset, personal growth and development

I have other important passions. In my spare time, I love kickboxing, hiking, camping, and long-distance running. I enjoy getting outdoors and encouraging others to do the same through my books and workbooks. These passions expanded out of my own personal growth journey.

While I did a bit of light hiking in high school, I was by no means athletic. I hated PE (physical education) classes with a passion, and I honestly thought I lacked the sporty gene. It wasn't until my late twenties that I started running, and it wasn't until my forties that I got into camping, kickboxing, and ultrarunning. My new and future interests include:

	Holly's Additional Interests
10	Kickboxing
11	Long-distance running
12	Hiking and backpacking
13	Camping
14	Creating books on nature and hiking

As you can see, my life has gone through various detours and pivots over the last three decades (changing countries and continents, what I did for a job and my hobbies and other interests), but a few things remained the same: my love for reading and writing and my love for nature and the outdoors. I've finally learned that it was possible to create a fulfilling life that combined many of my interests.

The most important takeaway from my journey was that it was a process of trial and error to get to where I am today. And it's still a work in progress.

I'm regularly re-evaluating my interests and priorities so I can ensure that I have the time to do the things that I most enjoy and that are most important to me. My life is not a template that I repeat year after year.

In terms of legacy, I think that will be my books about nature and hiking. Whether or not my podcast series will survive me remains to be seen, but it's likely that my books will. I hope that they will inspire people to get outdoors and connect with nature as part of their own personal growth and development journey.

If I were to reorganize these into similar categories, my UIS is then the sum of these items:

	Holly's Unique Interest Set
1	Reading
2	Writing books and blog posts
3	Nature, plants and trees
4	Spanish language
5	Travel
6	Helping authors
7	Podcasting and speaking
8	Kickboxing
9	Long-distance running
10	Hiking, backpacking and camping
11	Mindset, personal growth and development

Conclusion

Remember that creating a UIS like this is only Step 2 in the Dynamic Alignment process. In Step 3 and beyond, we will explain how to use a UIS list to create an inspiring path that is meaningful to you, the way Holly's is meaningful to her.

Brad's story

This is Brad. My story is different from Holly's and might serve as an example of how a UIS can work even when a person is employed by a large company.

From a young age, I had many interests. They stemmed from my high school days. One interest is modern things—new technology, modern art, and modern architecture. A second one is Antarctica—I've been fascinated by the stories of the early Antarctic explorers since I first read them as a young boy. I was mesmerized by their photographs of frozen landscapes. All I could think about was why would anyone want to go to such a cold and desolate place.

A third interest revolved around decision-making. Why do we make the decisions we make? What is good advertising, and does it really drive our behavior? What motivates our decision-making? Why do we have the relationships we engage in? As geeky as it may sound, I enjoyed watching TV ads and thinking about what message they were trying to convey.

A fourth was a desire to not lead the conventional life that seemed destined for me given my middle-class upbringing. And to somehow use that as a springboard to create something meaningful that would help others.

	Brad's Interests
1	Modern things / Modern technology
2	Antarctica
3	Decisions: Why do we do what we do?
4	Create something meaningful for others

I had a master's degree in Decision Sciences (the study of how businesses and people make decisions) from a leading university, but ironically made some poor decisions, including some bad relationship choices. Convinced that I was not smart enough to achieve a PhD, I left the university. The only good decision was I knew what I wanted—to work in a high-tech company and ultimately move from the US to London.

	Brad's Additional Interests
5	Working for high-tech companies
6	Living in the UK

At various points, I dabbled in all my interests, but it didn't all come together until 2015, shockingly late in my life. I worked in large software companies, dedicating myself to 60- to 70-hour weeks for years on end, as I tried to advance my career.

During that time, two new interests emerged:

	Brad's Additional Interests
7	Writing books: novels, non-fiction and self-help books
8	Being around creative people

Two of my passions, Antarctica and understanding the decisions people make, were not fulfilled. I couldn't get enough holiday time to go to Antarctica and I seemed destined to reach retirement age in a mid-level role in a very big company feeling like I never lived up to my potential. I was in my 50s when it was clear I had to make my own very big decision.

I was always surprised no one had written a book showcasing all of the life-and-death decisions the early Antarctic explorers made on the ice. In 2015, I decided I was the one to do it. To achieve this, I knew I needed a co-author, and I had to accept that I'd be working 15-16 hours per day—full-time for my employer and full-time on the book. I had previously written a novel that I didn't publish, so I knew I could do it if I could commit the time.

I found the right co-author, a historian named David Hirzel, and we spent two years writing and perfecting our book. The process opened many doors, meeting the most amazing people including acclaimed authors like Holly, and traveling to Antarctica twice.

Two additional interests emerged. One was writing more books about lessons from history, but this involved history beyond Antarctic explorers. The second was that as I became older, to live an active and productive life in the later years of my life.

In creating my current UIS I dropped some things and added others. It now looks like this:

	Brad's Unique Interest Set
1	Modern things
2	Antarctica
3	Decisions: Why do we do what we do?
4	Focusing on what modern people can learn from great people and endeavors in history (like the building of the Panama Canal or the invention of the airplane)
5	Using my experience to write self-help books
6	Being around creative people
7	Staying active and productive through later life and surrounding myself with other people who have a similar mindset

It's quite different from Holly's. It has 7 items compared to her 12 items. It's a bit wordier. As we said—there's no right or wrong. There's no set number of interests.

Now it's your turn

As you can see from our individual stories, Holly and Brad each have a unique combination of experiences (some good, some bad) and a variety of interests. Neither of us will probably ever meet another person with the exact same UIS.

You, too, have a particular set of knowledge, experience, and interests that no one else has. That is what the Life Factor Building Blocks proved. There is no one else on the planet like you. The trick now is to find and identify your combination of interests that uniquely thrill you.

Do this by looking at your Life Factor Building Blocks and considering them from the four perspectives of Past, Present, Future, and Your Legacy. Use these to identify what your areas of interest are.

Give it a try. It's fun to do. Add more rows if you need to.

	Your Interests
1	
2	
3	
4	
5	
6	

Ask yourself this:

Does your UIS characterize you, and when you think about the items on your list, do they energize you? If not, try writing them down differently (e.g. using different wording), reordering them, or starting again.

In the next chapter, we will explain Step 3, which involves looking at combinations of your interests in your UIS.

6

STEP 3: COMBINING ELEMENTS OF YOUR UIS

"The privilege of a lifetime is to become who you truly are."

— CARL JUNG

Armed with your Unique Interest Set, you can now decide how to best use it. This is Step 3 and is where the power of Dynamic Alignment starts to emerge.

Hopefully, your UIS uniquely defines you—you can always go back and refine it now or at any step in the process—and you can sense that you are the only person on the planet who can bring this unique combination of interests to life. The aim is that you perceive motivational power in this uniqueness.

You are no longer constrained by how society sees you or how others classify you.

Your uniqueness and the value you bring to society is embodied in your UIS. It's yours to own.

Even if you don't perceive that motivation yet, please continue to Steps 3 and 4, in this chapter and the next one.

Combinations

Step 3 in Dynamic Alignment is to look at your list not as a set of individual interests, but to use it to derive combinations of interests.

In a UIS list of say five interests—let's call them A, B, C, D and E—we can do an experiment. What would it look like if you combined four of them, for example A, B, C, and E? (We provide some specific examples below to illustrate how to do this.)

Now try another grouping of four of your five elements.

Do the same by combining three of them (A, C and D, for example), or two of them (such as just B and E). Even if they don't seemingly go together, let your mind wander in considering what various permutations would look like.

The greater the number of interests in your UIS, the more permutations are possible. Does doing this experiment spark any thoughts about what to do with these combinations? Does it inspire ways to monetize or sell services around any of your combinations or the entire UIS?

There are many ways to build a business or sell services around skill sets. Often this might involve starting small, or even starting with no identifiable income stream and little if any seed money to kickstart an initiative.

There's a variety of ways to use the UIS.

Job hunting: It now becomes much easier to explain your added value in any role you are applying for. Your uniqueness and capabilities may be exactly what a company is seeking. The UIS will help you distinguish yourself from other candidates. It can make you feel more confident.

Training others / tutoring / teaching: There may be people seeking to learn from someone with your skill set. You might have particular skills, as Holly does. She uses her publishing knowledge to help others write and publish books. You won't know until you try to engage in some type of training, tutoring, or teaching.

Consulting or mentoring: You may discover you have unique skills and experiences and others would benefit from learning from you. People might pay good money to learn what you know or do.

YouTube: A simple way to get started is to create some videos showcasing your uniqueness that others can learn from. Popular formats include how-to, instructional, and opinion videos. If being in front of a camera isn't your cup of tea, then you could write articles, blog posts, podcasts or other social content.

eBay/Etsy: Do you have expertise and interests in things that can be bought and sold on eBay or Etsy? For example, you may have a passion for unique, out-of-print books that could be collected and resold. Or maybe you're a skilled crocheter and could create intricate designs for sale. With your expertise or interests as defined in your UIS, you could start experimenting with either or both of these online platforms.

Value add: Do you have skills that enable you to take something that is already sold on the open market and add to it or embellish it in some way that adds further value, or increases its desirability to a specific group of people?

Step 4, in the next chapter, discusses some of these in more detail.

Brainstorm all combinations—here's an example

The key is to look at all permutations and think about how each would be monetized if you choose to do so. This should be a fun exploration of all your options and possibilities. Try to keep your mind open to new opportunities, even if they seem wild or impossible.

Let's take an example. Suppose your UIS looked like this:

	Example Unique Interest Set
1	Modern art
2	Clothing design
3	Writing short stories
4	Horses
5	Acting

Please note: If you think these items don't go together, remember a person's UIS is intended to be unique. It reflects that person's personality and interests, and should not be judged as inconsistent or improbable.

Here's the process of looking at combinations based on this UIS.

Firstly, look at groupings. What if you combined 1, 2, 3 and 4? Maybe that stimulates an idea or maybe not. How about 1, 3, 4, and 5? Or 2 and 4, which are: clothing design and horses.

There are so many variations when looking at this. Here are just a few.

1. Designing clothing with horse designs on the garments
2. Designing warm coats for horse owners/riders
3. Designing blankets for horses
4. Designing specialist clothing for horse riders or stable workers.

If you looked at 2, 3 and 4 as a combination—clothing design, writing short stories, horses:

	Example Combination
2	Clothing design
3	Writing short stories
4	Horses

What could you do with these interests?

It could involve writing short stories about horses, perhaps set in a stable where the rider's garment is an important part of the story.

Anything that picks up two or more elements of what interests you is more likely to be energizing enough to think about, and perhaps enough to try it.

The great thing about the internet is anything you create, you can promote. You can also sell via a platform like eBay (which is not just for used items), Amazon Marketplace, Etsy or through your own online store.

By combining your interests, you might be creating one-of-a-kind garments with horse images and selling them through your website, and offering short stories and blogs that you've written to attract attention from your potential audience.

To be interesting to you, it doesn't have to use all five elements. Maybe in this case, acting is not directly relevant, but perhaps your interest in modern art influences how you draw horses on clothing.

The more you brainstorm using your UIS, the more possibilities appear.

Don't fall into common traps

There are many common traps people fall into when brainstorming ideas that have the potential to be monetized.

1. "It's been done before."

It's easy to think this. Almost everything has been done before, yet there is always a market for quality, originality and a creative twist.

The other thing to remember is that if it has already been done, then that's proof there is a market for it. Just because a person has one of something doesn't mean they wouldn't like another of something similar. Proof of this is in shoes, clothing, books, sports equipment, souvenirs etc. People will happily own multiple examples of all of these things. It may have been done before, but it hasn't yet been done by you.

2. "No one would ever buy what I'm offering."

The best example is JK Rowling's Harry Potter books. Countless publishing houses turned down her first book, thinking, "No one would ever buy a book about a wizard." Over 600 million copies of her books have been sold. The greatest publishing companies in the world couldn't spot a blockbuster book. Try not to prejudge what people will do, say, or buy.

3. "I'm not an expert. Others know more."

Some people might know more but the key to brainstorming combined elements of your UIS and thinking about monetizing them is you are the one making it unique based on your experience, personality and interests, and in that, you become the expert.

No one else will do this combination exactly as you will— which means that others might respond to your way of doing things, and not the other person's.

4. "Someone else will do it better."

The sense of 'better' is subjective. What is better for one person is worse for someone else. The beauty of the world is we don't all share the same tastes and interests.

There are many examples where the 'better' item didn't become the popular item. This includes Microsoft Word, which at the time it was launched—and in its early years—was not any better than WordPerfect, which was the commonly used software at the time. Google was not initially better than Yahoo search—but it certainly evolved into the preferred search engine over time.

5. "I have little money or time."

Use your creativity. Some of the best ideas can be implemented for little cost. Building a sample or designing something on paper can be done quickly. If it matches your interests, then it's likely you will find a way to do it.

As for money, crowdfunding is one option that didn't exist

years ago, but has enabled thousands of creators to achieve their goals in recent years.

6. "Everyone says it's not possible."

Ignore the naysayers and critics. Every endeavor has its detractors. Teddy Roosevelt faced this throughout the construction of the Panama Canal. NASA faced this in the lead-up to the Apollo program to land a man on the Moon. It's far easier to be a critic than a doer, so it's best to ignore them.

Be confident that your unique experiences, personality and talents as shown in Step 1 (the Life Factor Building Blocks) combined with your UIS defined in Step 2, means that what you can define in Step 3 (Combinations of UIS elements) will be good or even great.

Refine as you go

As you go through this exercise, also be rethinking your UIS list. Have you missed anything? Could you word any of your UIS entries better?

In our example, perhaps the person might want to change number 5 from 'Acting' to 'Making videos'. The question to ask yourself when making a change is: Does that change what interests you? Are you more interested in the creative process of acting, appearing on screen, or both?

You also might find it useful to get feedback from a close friend or partner. Sometimes, it's hard to see ourselves clearly and outside feedback can be helpful.

Maybe number 1 should be renamed 'Modern design', not 'Modern art'.

Or it's not a 'replace,' but an additional element in your UIS, so your UIS now has seven items.

	Example Unique Interest Set - refined
1	Modern art
2	Modern design
3	Clothing design
4	Writing short stories
5	Horses
6	Acting
7	Creating and editing videos

Make your UIS authentically you

The more you experiment and test your UIS, the more you will be able to create something specific to your personality and interests.

You might think lots of people like modern art and design, writing, acting and creating videos, clothing design, and horses. That may be true. Two actions are needed.

The first is to revisit your UIS and strive to make it more true to you. Look at each element and enhance it. What is it about horses that you like? What were your first experiences riding or caring for them, or is your focus in seeing them grazing or envisioning what they were like in the days of the Wild West in the USA in the 1800s?

In terms of short stories, be more specific. What types of short stories do you like - romantic comedies, thrillers, detective stories, etc? What types don't you like?

The second action is to add or subtract from your UIS list. What else could you add to make it more tailored to you? What are you less passionate about that could be dropped from the list? Your focus has to be to make your UIS authentically represent you.

The more the UIS authentically matches you, the more useful it will be.

This brings us to the next step: Step 4, which we call Dabbling.

7

STEP 4: THE HIDDEN POWER OF DABBLING

"Life isn't about finding yourself. Life is about creating yourself."

— *GEORGE BERNARD SHAW*

There are several schools of thought about undertaking new endeavors.

There's a belief that to undertake something new you must throw yourself into the deep end—the best way to learn and achieve is through full immersion. The idea is that you must fully, 100 percent, commit to something: "Don't quit till you've achieved it."

There's another school of thought which holds that you have to fully research everything you do before you do it. "You have to think before you leap and try things out."

Both of these approaches have their merits for certain endeavors, but when the time comes to start thinking about monetizing your UIS, we'd like to propose an alternative approach. We call it, "The hidden power of dabbling."

> Dabbling is the simple art of "trying it." Borrowing from
> Nike's well-conceived slogan, "Just Do It."

When you're considering something new don't overthink it, just give it a try! Play around with it and see if you enjoy it. You don't need to commit 100 percent, nor do you need to spend months doing market research. Just dabble. That's Step 4 in Dynamic Alignment.

Armed with your list of combinations derived from your UIS, what combinations of interests inspire you enough to try one of them?

The easiest way to explain it is with examples

If you have an interest in being an antiques dealer, you could dabble at selling some antiques at a car boot sale as they are called in the UK, or doing a yard or garage sale if you live in the US. Or buy and sell some antiques on eBay. Or do both yard sales and eBay sales. We know people who have done this, and successfully transitioned to become full-time antiques, book and ephemera (printed historical documents) dealers and are doing very well.

The more you dabble at things, the more opportunities you will discover. The trick is to keep an open mind. Talk with people already in that field. Start small and keep asking yourself if you are enjoying it.

Using our own examples, Holly had a desire to run ultramarathons. Running can't be experienced from a textbook or YouTube video. You have to experience actual long-distance running. It's as simple as lacing up some sneakers or running shoes, grabbing a water bottle, and getting outside and running.

Is it pleasurable? If it is, then you keep it in your UIS. However, running around the block outside your house is far different from running an ultramarathon, which is different from running a shorter race. Through dabbling, Holly could do some running, think, "Yes, I enjoy this," and enter herself in a race far enough in the future to enable her to train for it.

Perhaps by dabbling with short races, she'd think, "I enjoy running, but not running timed races against competitors." Alternatively, she might be revitalized by the racing experience and become more motivated to enter races of longer distances. She couldn't know for certain until she tried it.

Another example is when Brad started to brainstorm his first co-authored book on the life-and-death decisions made by the early Antarctic explorers. Several people said he needed to do detailed research on 'the competition' —other books about the explorers—before putting pen to paper.

Brad and his co-author, David Hirzel, decided on a different approach - one akin to dabbling. They decided to first work on the issues of: Could they work well together since they lived 8 time zones apart? Would Brad enjoy the writing process? (David was already a published author.) Did they have a message worth conveying? All of this could be learned by a few weeks of dabbling—brainstorming a table of contents, discussing who would write what, and creating a few writing samples, and then co-writing an article together. They did this all before ever committing to write an entire book together.

Dabbling is inexpensive

Dabbling is inexpensive. It's quick. It doesn't commit you to anything. You can make it fun. It's a 'try it' approach, with little downside.

You might dabble in something and decide it's not for you. Or it's for you, but not in the way you had initially envisioned. Or it could lead to something bigger if the endeavor was shaped differently.

You might think of it as:

1. Dabble
2. Assess your result. Was it good enough? Did you enjoy it?
3. Tweak what you did
4. Dabble again ... and so on.

Dabbling also lets you exercise detachment. With less investment, it's easier to cut loose and try something else. You're not committed to it.

The more you experiment with dabbling the more you can test your UIS and all the various combinations of how you mix and match different elements from your UIS.

The ultimate goal is to find ways to monetize groupings of elements from your UIS so that when undertaking them, they are *so* energizing to you they don't feel like work. Plus they give you a purpose and a drive because it's only you, with all the uniqueness of you revealed in your Life Factor Building Blocks, who can deliver on the combinations derived from your UIS.

Friends, colleagues and the internet can help

The power of the internet can help improve your dabbling. Using Google, YouTube, eBay, Amazon Marketplace, Etsy and other sources you can learn how to create markets, find opportunities or jobs, find and reach potential clients, build websites, and find groups and individuals with similar interests.

Use your UIS to broaden your thoughts as to what interests you and what makes you specifically unique. Then use friends, colleagues and the internet to come up with ways you might monetize all or part of your UIS, and then start dabbling.

Try it. It might reveal a new and exciting endeavor in your life and career.

A more structured approach

You could take a more structured approach. For every combination of elements from your UIS that you think could have potential, brainstorm two or three ways you could dabble in it. Then try some of them.

As you do this you might find new interests to add to your UIS, or interests that are not strong enough to remain in your UIS. Steps 2, 3 and 4 can be used interchangeably and repeatedly until you discover something that is thrilling enough to pursue more.

8

STEP 5: YOUR UNIQUE GOAL
SETTING STYLE

> *"Without dreams and goals there is no living, only merely existing, and that is not why we are here."*
>
> — *MARK TWAIN*

One of the many benefits of creating a UIS and examining all the possible combinations of interests within it is that it reveals the variety of things that energize you. A challenge for people is then to avoid losing focus on which things and combinations are the most motivational ones. They all might sound exciting.

The solution: goals. Set goals so you aren't just drifting through life. Goals help to ensure that you are prioritizing what you want to do.

If you don't like the word 'goals,' think of them as 'desires.'

Goal setting or determining desires may sound daunting, so we recommend making Step 5 of Dynamic Alignment as easy to define as possible using an approach we developed.

Everyone has their own unique style of setting goals and working towards them. That's due to a combination of individual differences, experiences, and personality traits. Each person has unique values, aspirations, desires and priorities that shape their goal-setting process.

Diverse life experiences greatly impact how people approach goal-setting. Past successes and failures, as well as the lessons learned along the way, can mold a person's goal-setting style. Someone who has faced significant setbacks in the past might adopt a more cautious and incremental approach to setting goals, while a person who has consistently achieved their targets may set more ambitious and daring objectives.

The cultural, familial, and societal influences that individuals are exposed to can also contribute to shaping their goal-setting styles. Different cultural norms and expectations may place emphasis on certain types of goals, influencing individuals to adopt particular approaches to goal-setting and achievement. And factors like self-efficacy, optimism, and perseverance can influence a person's ability to stay committed to their goals and overcome obstacles along the way.

Personality traits and cognitive factors play a crucial role in shaping how individuals approach their goals.

Some people are naturally more inclined towards meticulous planning, breaking down tasks into smaller steps, and setting deadlines, which allows for a more structured and organized approach to goal achievement. On the other hand, people who are more spontaneous and adaptable may prefer setting flexible goals and embracing opportunities as they arise, leading to a more fluid and dynamic goal-setting style.

As with every other aspect of Dynamic Alignment, it's important to find what works for you.

Identifying your Goal Language

Just like a person is said to have a love language—a way a person wants others to express romantic love to them, we believe each person has a Goal Language.

Rather than this being externally linked, it is an internal language. It's how you express goals to yourself that resonate with you and can motivate your behavior.

Be clear on what you want

Setting vague or unclear goals can lead to confusion, making it difficult to measure progress. There are many approaches to setting goals: some are rigid, and others are more flexible. They'll both get you to the same place, but the approach is different.

The key is to find what works best for you, based on what resonates with you. In the different goal-setting approaches, the motivating force varies. You'll want to decide what you find more motivating: the journey or the end goal.

A goal can be as simple as writing down one sentence, or even half a sentence that answers the question: "What do you want to achieve?"

Below, we'll share with you two common ways of setting goals. It helps that Brad and Holly have very different styles, so we can explain with personal examples.

Brad's approach

Brad prefers to focus on the journey toward achieving the goal, rather than the end goal itself. Here's Brad's take on goals. It's a methodology for those who are less goals-focused. He calls it SEES.

A goal should be:

- Simple to articulate.
- Easy to remember.
- Easy to achieve.
- You can also include Stretch goals if you like.

Let's dive into each of these aspects.

Simple to articulate: For people like Brad, keep your goals simple. Goals should be easy to articulate in a single phrase, such as "I want to plan a week-long, solo trip to Norway."

Easy to remember: This is so you can keep your goal at the forefront of your mind. "I want to plan a week-long, solo trip to Norway" is great, because it's easy to remember without getting bogged down in all the little details of where you want to go when you get there.

Easy to achieve: If you are someone who is driven by success and enjoys ticking things off lists, why not set easy goals? A week-long, solo trip is a great goal for someone who isn't an experienced traveler. If you choose a popular tourist destination, there will be plenty of online resources to plan the trip, and it will be easy to create an itinerary that works with your budget.

Stretch yourself: You can add in stretch goals—and these stretch goals can also be on a sliding scale. You can decide if these stretch goals will be relatively easy, challenging or extremely challenging to achieve. You can also add a time limit or a deadline to your goal if that helps you to stretch yourself.

For example, you might stretch yourself to a two-week trip involving multiple destinations or to a more adventurous location. Or you might plan to take a sabbatical from work and go on a three-month or year-long trip around the world.

If you want to set a deadline, you can adjust the goal as follows: "I want to plan a week-long, solo trip to Norway by the end of next year."

Holly's approach

Holly's approach to goals is quite different. Holly uses a loose variation of the SMART goal approach, which is a concept that you may be familiar with since it is widely used in business.

SMART stands for Specific, Measurable, Achievable, Relevant, and Time-Bound. While she doesn't go through each of the five steps to ensure that the goal is SMART, she does set a very specific goal with a deadline.

Deadlines are an important part of this approach for Holly. She found that without a deadline, it can be harder to work toward her goal. That's one of the reasons why having an event like a race or a kickboxing grading helps her to do the training she needs to do to achieve the goal.

Let's say you want to run a 5K race. One example of a SMART goal is this: "I will complete a 5K race within the next three months." Let's break this down into five parts.

Specific: The goal specifies a clear objective, which is to complete a 5K race. It is specific about the desired outcome. It's not just any race of any distance.

Measurable: The goal is measurable because you're aiming to complete a 5K race that has a specific distance to cover.

Achievable: The goal is realistic and achievable for many individuals with average fitness levels. It's a great first race. It considers the individual's capabilities, resources, and time frame.

Relevant: The goal is relevant to the person's desire to improve their fitness and participate in a specific event (the 5K race). It aligns with their personal interests and goals.

Time-bound: The goal has a defined time frame of three months, providing a specific deadline for completion. You can then go online and find a 5K race sometime in the next 3 months that fits into your schedule. Without a deadline, goals often don't happen.

Are these really your goals?

Part of the process is to assess if these really are your passions, as you grow and change and as the world evolves around you. What you may desire one year, may not be desired the next year. The world is moving too fast for us to be fully fixated on a small set of unchanging must-do goals. That's why we called this process Dynamic Alignment—it is an ever-evolving process.

We know of at least three different people who had promising careers as musicians, playing in bands well-known enough that you would likely know their music if it came up on a Spotify playlist, yet once they had children on the way, realized that they needed to move away from their passion and goal of being in a band that toured the world to a life of working a steadier job with less travel.

One went back to university to learn computer programming. One became a business executive. And one began producing his own music. The first two never left behind their passion for music, they just moved to different primary goals that gave them the stable life they desired.

And before anyone says, computer programming sounds boring, please remember this is their passion, and for him, it really was a passion. People can have passions for just about anything and it is good to accept that your passions aren't theirs and theirs aren't yours.

We knew a hairdresser in suburban London who ran his own successful salon with loyal staff and customers. The owner discovered that he enjoyed the accounting side of the business far more than the hairdressing work. He ultimately sold his hairdressing salon and joined as a junior member of another salon to help pay the bills so he could take accounting and bookkeeping courses. He has now given up hairdressing completely and works in accounting.

To each his or her own. It's not for us to judge that owning a salon would be more fun than accounting. Accounting was this person's passion.

In fact, we'd advocate that by taking a Dynamic Alignment approach, he might become more successful and more fulfilled by combining his passion for the hairdressing business with his passion for accountancy and focusing on providing accounting services to London-based hairdressers.

What is your goal language?

In summary, start by determining what your goal language is. What motivates you—easy goals quickly attained or harder goals? Whatever your style, make the goals relevant to you. You choose the timescale and the difficulty level. You can make them easy-to-achieve milestones or hard-to-achieve, out-of-your-comfort-zone goals.

Whether you choose Brad's SEES approach or Holly's SMART approach, or create your own unique style of goals, the key is alignment to what motivates you to move forward in your Dynamic Alignment journey.

9

STEP 6: TAKE ACTION. PURSUE DYNAMICALLY ALIGNED MULTI-PASSIONATE GOALS

"Dare mighty things."

— *THEODORE ROOSEVELT*

The power of Dynamic Alignment is that this is personal to *you*. When you've defined your Unique Interest Set, identified combinations of elements from your UIS and brainstormed how to bring them to life, and then dabbled in making them a reality you are well on your way. Identifying goals can show you a path forward.

Step 6 is about taking action. Pursuing your goals, however you define them—short term, long term, easy, hard, whatever style you choose, the key is moving forward towards them.

While some people might feel more comfortable pursuing one goal at a time, to realize the power of Dynamic Alignment, we'd like to encourage you to pursue multiple goals, all at the same time.

There are a number of reasons for this. You may decide one of the goals is no longer interesting or motivating to you. Multiple goals can reinforce one another, such as our example of Holly's pursuit of kickboxing achievement goals, ultramarathon goals, hiking goals, and writing books about her hikes.

What we have found in people pursuing what we call Dynamically Aligned Multi-Passionate Goals is there's power in doing it.

There's a sense of fulfillment and inner happiness, even contentment, in defining, knowing and using the skills, talents, interests and experiences that are uniquely yours.

You might initially think pursuing multiple goals all at the same time would be tiring. We have found the exact opposite— it is energizing. It keeps you focused. Actions that you take in pursuit of one of your goals may prove useful in pursuit of some of your other goals, so there's a synergy that can happen as well.

Ignore the naysayers

When undertaking this approach be aware of people who seek 'to rain on your parade.'

Naysayers, people who say, 'It can't be done,' and critics are not to be listened to when pursuing your interests and goals.

It is surprising how many experts told Marc Brunel, an internationally renowned engineer, and his son Isambard Kingdom Brunel who later went on to be probably the greatest engineer who ever lived, that they would never be able to build a tunnel under the River Thames in London. The tunnel took longer to build than originally planned, and it still exists today, over 170 years later.

Many people told Roald Amundsen that he'd never be able to find the sea route across northern Canada called the Northwest Passage—a sea route sought for over 400 years—because he was planning to do it in a 70-foot boat with 6 other men—so a very small boat with a very small crew. Amundsen had done his research and knew he could accomplish it.

Naysayers are all around us. Why? Because it's cheap and easy to criticize other people's efforts. When you are pursuing your interests and goals and you feel you are on the correct path, tune out the critics and focus on those people who are supportive of your efforts and who believe you will make a success of your endeavors.

A dynamic approach

Remember, this is a *dynamic* approach. You can evolve this approach as you grow and mature. You can have multiple UISs and Multi-Passionate Goals throughout your lifetime. You can gain new life experiences, pick up new hobbies and interests, drop others, dabble in many things, and add to and update your goals at any time.

At a minimum, you can take the approach that the UIS you define now may be different five years from now, and very likely different again in ten years.

Rethinking the combinations and goals revealed from your UIS is always a valuable exercise.

The key is that when you are dynamically aligned between your Life Factor Building Blocks, your UIS and the combinations of its elements that energize you, all of that along with any goals you've defined along the way gives you the motivation to get started and keep going.

One of the reasons it is likely that your Multi-Passionate Goals will evolve is that more doors will open and more opportunities will be revealed to you as you pursue your UIS interests and goals. We call this phenomenon: Life Magnetism. This is Step 7 and the benefits of it are explained in the next chapter.

10

STEP 7: LIFE MAGNETISM

> *"Encourage yourself, believe in yourself, and love yourself. Never doubt who you are."*
>
> — *STEPHANIE LAHART*

When we started our discussions about goals that led to this book, one of the things we were both struck by was:

As you start focusing on achieving your dynamically aligned multi-passionate goals, you begin to attract people, resources and opportunities that help you achieve them.

This is a phenomenon that we both experienced and we heard of from a number of people.

Two things were happening. One was that we were each more attuned to spotting opportunities related to our goals. The other was more opportunities seemed to arise as we were embarking on the journey of pursuing our own multi-passionate goals.

This seemed reminiscent of a quote from the Jason Bourne books by Robert Ludlum. In one of the books, Jason Bourne can't fully remember his own past but he knows one thing for certain:

> *"Opportunities will present themselves. Recognize them, act on them."*
> —*Jason Bourne*

Jason Bourne may be a fictional character, but his sentiment is easy to understand. One of the keys to achieving your goals is both recognizing opportunities and, equally important, trusting yourself to take full advantage of any opportunities you spot. The more we know who we are and what we are seeking, the clearer opportunities become, and also the braver we can be in pursuing them.

Our own experiences showed that doors open that never would have opened before, both figuratively and literally. Opportunities included networking with people, meeting people far above our stature whom we would never have met in our previous social and business circles, and learning valuable skills from many others.

It's also possible to attract funding, sponsors and other outside assistance in your pursuit of goals. Efforts in dabbling paid off, not always in monetary terms, but in terms of learning experiences and often, even if they failed, led to something bigger and better.

The fun is that this starts to feel like empowerment and that can lead to a more enriching life.

Why does Life Magnetism work?

Life Magnetism works for a myriad of reasons. It could be that in pursuing your own uniqueness, you give off a sense of purpose. People like to be around other people who have a sense of where they are going and why they are aiming for it. It adds to your depth of character and it reveals to others that you are a motivated person who can be stimulating and interesting to be around.

Having a purpose gives you an inner strength that means you may no longer be shy or reserved in talking with strangers or asking people for help, guidance or mentoring. It also means you are willing to share what you are doing, why you are doing it, and what specifically you need. Another rule of the universe we discovered: the more you share, the more you get back in return.

Another element of why Life Magnetism works is people are attracted to helping those who know what they are seeking.

A listless, unmotivated person can be draining to be around. A person who is dynamically aligned and knows that their UIS matches their authentic self is likely to be more energized, more full of life, and more fun to have a conversation with.

It also works because it can feel like the universe is aligning to help you achieve—or move you closer to achieving—your multi-passionate goals. We aren't sure about 'aligning the universe' but what is probably happening is you are displaying a sense of confidence and focus and are then more attuned to reading situations and meeting people who have a similar interest or the means or connections to help you.

All in all, people, resources and opportunities will present themselves. Be ready to watch for that. As Jason Bourne knows, "Recognize them. Act on them."

Work no longer feels like work

In addition to Life Magnetism, another outcome of pursuing your multi-passionate goals is that work no longer feels like work. It is synonymous with you taking on endeavors that uniquely speak to your talents.

Since the Life Magnetism you experience is based on your UIS, only you can deliver the multi-passionate goals. In that regard, they are energizing. If only you can do something or achieve something, then it becomes meshed with your personality, your sense of purpose and something you 'own' when it is accomplished.

Also, in this regard, the journey to attain or achieve becomes fun, and not synonymous with endeavors you had previously undertaken that you might have seen as strenuous, stressful or onerous.

The end result is that by identifying and working on your own multi-passionate goals, you have a strong motivator for getting out of bed feeling energized or revitalized, and working towards successful outcomes. It's your journey. It's your goals that are being pursued. It's your success if and when they are achieved.

11

STEP 8: EVOLVING YOUR DYNAMICALLY ALIGNED MULTI-PASSIONATE LIFE

"If you don't like the road you're walking, start paving another one."

— *DOLLY PARTON*

Your multi-passionate goals and all the steps you've taken to define your dynamically aligned life do not have to be 'one and done.' Every aspect can be reassessed at any time as you—and the world around you—evolve. That's why the word Dynamic is as important as the word Alignment in our process.

Early in this book, we described your Life Factor Building Blocks as being like a unique set of fingerprints. While they uniquely define you, unlike fingerprints which stay with you for life, the Life Factor Building Blocks evolve because your attitudes and perceptions result from a set of skills, talents and experiences that you are constantly adding to.

As you gain new experiences and insights you may find a different UIS fits you better. From that UIS you can define new combinations, engage in different types of dabbling, identify new goals, and do this as you grow and age. Also, Life

Magnetism may come into play, and those opportunities, people and resources you've attracted into your life may encourage or inspire you to make adjustments to the Dynamic Alignment process.

How often you check in and reevaluate your UIS and goals is up to you. It's something that could be done monthly, quarterly, or annually. You can also update your goals on an ad-hoc basis, whenever one of them has stopped being meaningful. You don't need to wait until a scheduled check-in to adjust it.

We expect that you will have learned from the process and will be able to go through it faster, quicker and better each time. There will be elements you will find you want to drop out of your UIS, and others to be added in.

You will become more skilled in finding the words to define your UIS, and in looking at the various combinations of its elements to pinpoint the ones that truly energize you.

It's important to keep your eyes on your own lane. Try to avoid comparing yourself with others. Everyone's journey is different, and even armed with your UIS and multi-passionate goals, it's easy to fall into the trap of comparing yourself with friends, relatives, strangers and people you read about or see in social media. Instead, focus on your own goals and aspirations and everything that makes you uniquely valuable, and then take steps towards achieving what inspires you.

We posed three questions at the start of the book:

1. Why is it that some people wake up energized, raring to go, enthralled with all the challenges ahead?
2. What is it that these people have in common?
3. Can it be encapsulated into a formula that anyone can use today?

The answer is to uncover your own uniqueness, discover your own Unique Interest Set, derive your multi-passionate goals from various combinations of your UIS elements, and look for all those Life Magnetism opportunities that come your way so you can take advantage of them. Pursue what thrills you for the positive betterment of yourself and the world.

Celebrate your successes when getting near to them or achieving them, learn from setbacks and obstacles, and revisit your UIS and multi-passionate goals regularly.

And most of all, we hope that these methods enable you to feel energized or revitalized and empowered to do what you are uniquely capable of achieving.

Now that you know the process, the next chapter encourages you to get started.

12

TIPS FOR GETTING STARTED TODAY

> *"Ignore your mistakes. The number one thing to worry about is: Am I doing what I'm good at?"*
>
> — *MAX LEVCHIN, CO-FOUNDER OF THE COMPANY*
> *THAT BECAME PAYPAL*

An important part of the Dynamic Alignment process is moving from reading about it to getting started doing it. Whether you leave the starting blocks with small steps or by taking giant ones, the key is to get started and then keep going. And you can do that soon, even today.

While this book can be read from cover to cover, it serves its real purpose when it compels you to think and take action. It's not meant to be a motivational or inspirational self-help book where you read it and feel better about your life, because that's just temporary. Our goal is to help you make positive, empowering, revitalizing, energizing changes and choices that match your authentic self. How can you do that?

The basic steps are defined in the chapter sequence and description of the steps. Start by re-reading through the Life

Factor Building Blocks and thinking about the categories and elements. The more time you spend doing this the more you will realize and appreciate your unique importance and value. No one else on the planet has experienced what you have, nor does anyone have your set of attitudes, beliefs, abilities, desires and perceptions. Those elements, when applied to your interests and motivations, become an unstoppable force for good.

You can use our workbook, which will walk you through each step of the process, or create your own dedicated notebook or journal. If you prefer keeping things online, then open up a notes app or document on your phone, tablet, or computer, and make notes there.

Next, try listing your UIS. What's in it? What's definitely not in it? Make notes using whatever system you prefer (our workbook, your own notebook, journal, Word document, Google doc, Notes app, etc.) to document your response.

Write down your UIS and ask yourself, "How does this feel to me?" Does it match the authentic you, or do things need to be added? Adjust your UIS as needed. Try again, recognizing it might take many iterations to get a UIS that matches your authentic self and is also so inspiring and motivational that it thrills you when you read the entries. Then explore your combinations based on elements in your UIS and brainstorm how you could use dabbling to bring them to fruition as a test to determine their effectiveness and value.

Remember, this process doesn't need to be done in one sitting.

In fact, you'll probably benefit from getting started, and then adding to your LFBBs and UIS from time to time.

Here are a few tips to help you along the way.

Set realistic expectations

Setting realistic expectations can lead to satisfying achievements. Setting overly ambitious goals can result in frustration and disappointment.

For example, let's say that after going through the Dynamic Alignment process, you come up with the goal to write a memoir by the end of the year—but you've never written a book or published an article before. That can be a daunting project especially with this tight deadline, which means that the goal probably isn't realistic without more structure, such as defining some intermediary goals or milestones.

It is up to you whether you delve right in or spend time studying how other memoirs are put together, structured, written and marketed. Whichever method you use, inspiration and dedication are key. Nothing is done easily and simply just because you want it to be.

We even fell into this dilemma in brainstorming and working on this book. Our expectation as experienced writers was that we could create it in three to six months. It has taken well over a year, with many rewrites along the way to create this short book.

Setting goals

As we discussed in Step 5, everyone has their own unique goal language, style of setting goals, and working toward them. This individuality stems from a blend of personal differences, life experiences, and personality traits. Each person possesses distinct values, aspirations, and priorities that shape their approach to setting goals.

Life's diverse experiences significantly influence how people embark on their goal-setting journeys. Past triumphs and setbacks, along with the wisdom gained from them, shape one's style of goal setting. Those who have encountered formidable obstacles might lean toward a cautious, step-by-step approach, while those with a track record of achievements may set audacious objectives. Cultural, familial, and societal factors also play a role in shaping these styles, as they can emphasize certain goals and approaches.

Furthermore, personality traits and cognitive factors influence how individuals approach their goals; some lean towards meticulous planning and structure, while others prefer flexibility and adaptability. Whether following Brad's SEES approach, Holly's preferred SMART method, or crafting a unique style, the key is aligning your goals with your values and motivations to pave the path toward success. Find what works for you.

Align your goals to your values

To aid success, make sure that your goals align with your authentic values which are defined by your Life Factor Building Blocks exercise.

When your goals are dynamically aligned to your unique self, they're fun to work towards.

On the other hand, pursuing goals that are not aligned with your core values and passions can lead to a lack of fulfillment and motivation. When your goals are misaligned, it makes it much harder to achieve them.

Remember to reflect on your LFBBs and UIS and align your goals with them, reassess your priorities, and make necessary adjustments to find fulfillment in your pursuits.

Also, as time goes on, if a goal no longer makes sense to you, change it.

Nothing in this process needs to be cast in stone. Adjust it to meet your personality and needs.

Create a plan

This tip is related to the previous point. When you have a clear plan and you work on it, you're more likely to achieve your goals. Conversely, failing to create a plan with specific actions and milestones can make it challenging to make progress toward your goals. The key is creating a plan that matches your style of planning.

If you like detailed plans that are written down, that is fine. If you find that style of planning daunting, write a simpler plan or just create a plan in your head. We recommend writing it down if you can. Even a simple plan consisting of a few bullet points on paper, in an app, or in your mind, is better than no plan.

If you have a goal of running a 5K race, that's probably not something most people can just wake up and do. That's why there are so many "Couch to 5K" training programs. And if you've signed up for a longer race, there will be even more training involved. Plan all the steps you need to take to achieve the goal, and in this case, it will involve getting out of your home to run on a regular basis - even when it's cold and dreary outside.

Create an action plan adding as much or as little detail as you like to outline the steps, timelines, and resources needed to achieve your goals.

Commit to your goals

There has to be some level of commitment to your goals. When you're committed, it makes it easier to take action.

Without a strong commitment to your goals, it's more likely that you will give up when faced with obstacles.

That's why it's so important to choose multi-passionate goals that are important to *you*, not to other people. Make sure that they are aligned to your values. If you're going to dedicate valuable time, effort, and perhaps money, to your goals, you want to be sure you truly want them.

Sometimes, we lose commitment along the way—especially when they're big projects. We forget our initial reason for wanting to achieve the goal. That's why it's important to check in with our goals regularly and ensure they're still right for us.

Find your motivation and purpose behind the goals, remind yourself of them regularly, and create a support system to stay accountable.

Share your goals with others

When you share your goals with other people, it makes it easier to achieve them. Plus, it can be fun to share your plans with friends and family who are supportive of your dreams and desires. When we share our goals with others, it helps us to do the things we need to do in order to achieve them.

You can share your goals with trusted friends and family members who can provide support and encouragement—and even help you check and assess your progress. This also relates to the Life Magnetism concept described earlier in the book.

You never know who can help you achieve your goals, and what we have found is that it's surprising how many people, resources and opportunities exist to help you, once you reveal to people what you are trying to do.

Celebrate!

Something that is easy to ignore is the importance of acknowledging and celebrating your milestones as you achieve them. It can help with motivation and satisfaction, especially when your goals and projects are big or they are stretch goals. Sometimes, it can feel like a long journey to achieve our goals.

That's why it's so important to celebrate even the small wins: you need to acknowledge everything you've achieved.

When you take a moment to look back toward where you were at Point A, you'll see all the things you've done along the way: all the actions you've taken and all the things you've achieved so far. It can be motivating and inspiring and will help you continue to take action toward your goals.

Acknowledge and reward yourself for achieving milestones, practice gratitude, share your successes with others, and take time to reflect on your progress.

The benefit of all this effort is creating your multi-passionate legacy. This is explained in the next chapter.

13

YOUR MULTI-PASSIONATE LEGACY

> *"It will never rain roses: when we want to have more roses, we must plant more roses."*
>
> — *GEORGE ELIOT*

There is a big side benefit to defining your UIS and pursuing your dynamically aligned multi-passionate goals, and this has to do with your legacy.

Even at a young age, it is useful to think of what sort of mark you'd wish to leave on the world.

How would you like to be remembered? What will your friends, family, and even complete strangers say about you when reading about your life ten, fifty or a hundred years from now?

Your Life Factor Building Blocks will give you some answers to this, as will your UIS. People who pursue multi-passionate goals seem to instinctively know that doing so will be part of their legacy—a dynamically aligned legacy.

Identify your legacy vision

Start by reflecting on your aspirations: explore what legacy means to you personally. Is it important to you? It's okay if it's not—not everyone is concerned with leaving a legacy.

Envision the future, and think about how you would like to be remembered. What would be the impact you'd wish to have made on the world? Who do you want to benefit from your legacy? Who will be helped by it?

Define your legacy goals: set specific objectives that align with your multi-passionate interests and contribute to your desired legacy. Then, work toward them using the process we've outlined in previous chapters.

Embrace your unique LFBBs

Continue to work on discovering and understanding your Life Factor Building Blocks: identify the key elements of your life. You could add them to a workbook or journal or just hold them as thoughts in your head.

Recognize the power of your uniqueness by reviewing your UIS and the combinations of the elements within it so you can understand how unique you are and use those experiences to fuel your multi-passionate pursuits. Leverage your strengths by determining how to use your unique qualities and experiences to create a legacy that truly resonates with your authentic self.

Unleash the power of your multi-passionate goals

Embrace the synergy of your passions by exploring how pursuing your multiple passions can contribute to a richer, more meaningful legacy. How can they work together to create your unique legacy?

You can even set dynamically aligned multi-passionate goals that relate to your legacy. Establish new, specific goals that integrate your various passions, allowing you to make a lasting impact in different areas of your life.

Adjust your journey along the way by reflecting on your purpose and fulfillment. Does aligning your multi-passionate goals with your legacy vision bring a sense of purpose and fulfillment to your life? If not, adjust your goals and work toward your legacy in a different way.

Nurture your legacy through action

Break down your legacy goals into actionable steps and consistently pursue them, keeping an eye out for any bumps in the road along the way. Overcome these challenges and setbacks by focusing on your motivational drivers.

Seek out support and collaboration if needed. Remember, when you engage with like-minded individuals, mentors, and communities you can gain valuable encouragement, guidance, and collaboration opportunities. Also, don't forget the power and synergy that will come from Life Magnetism.

Leave a lasting impact: your multi-passionate legacy

Live your legacy now by embracing the idea that your legacy is not only something to be left behind but also something to embody and live in the present. There's a lot you can do now to nurture your legacy.

Inspire others by sharing your story, experiences, and insights to motivate and empower others to embrace their own multi-passionate journeys.

This can also create a ripple effect: you'll recognize the

potential for your multi-passionate legacy to create a positive impact that extends beyond your immediate sphere of influence. This can also spur you to expand and amplify your existing legacy.

We wish you extraordinary success on your journey.

THE 8 STEPS

1. Identify your Life Factor Building Blocks
2. Define your UIS
3. Look at all the different ways you can combine your various interests to create different and compelling career and life paths.
4. Dabbling
5. Goals and Goal language
6. Pursue your goals
7. Look out for opportunities arising from synergy, which we call Life Magnetism.
8. On-going Dynamic alignment

A NOTE TO OUR READERS

If you enjoyed this book, we would be most grateful for a review on Amazon, Goodreads or any other sites that readers might visit. It takes just a couple of minutes to write a short review. It would mean the world to us! Reviews help other readers to discover our books.

Thank you!
Brad and Holly

RECOMMENDED RESOURCES

Here are the two podcast episodes with Holly and Brad that inspired this book. The numbers refer to the number of each podcast episode:

- 471 Goal Setting for Adventures and Life (now with downloadable transcript!)
- 422 Adventures in Audacious Goal Setting

And here's a list of the most relevant episodes from Holly's podcast that relate to this book. For more episodes, search for "*Into the Woods with Holly Worton*" on your favorite podcast app or visit Holly's website: http://hollyworton.com/podcast.

- 490 Holly Worton – How Bad Do You Want It? Finding Motivation For Your Adventures (now with downloadable transcript!)
- 485 Marie-Pier Tremblay ~ How To Go After Big Dreams And Adventures, Even When You Think It's Impossible

- 476 Holly Worton ~ How to Know When Enough is Enough With Your Hobbies and Adventure
- 467 Holly Worton ~ Hike Your Own Hike, On The Trail And In Life
- 463 Holly Worton ~ There's No Failure, Only Feedback: When Our Adventures Go "Wrong"
- 459 Holly Worton ~ How to Know When You're Putting Too Much Pressure on Yourself
- 456 Jenny Mowbray ~ How to Fund Your Adventures With a Flexible Portfolio Career (now with downloadable transcript!)
- 452 Diane Randall ~ Putting More Life into Your Work-Life Balance
- 448 Dominique Brightmon ~ 5 Keys for Elite Performance in Adventure and Life
- 447 Jen Ruiz ~ How to Balance Travel and Adventure With a Full-Time Job

DYNAMIC ALIGNMENT WORKBOOK

In order to help you work your way through our 8-step Dynamic Alignment process, we've created a workbook. It includes each of the 8 steps, and expands upon many of the questions that will help you to determine your Life Factor Building Blocks.

It's available as a paperback on Amazon and other major online booksellers.

HOW WE CAN HELP YOU

Need help working through our Dynamic Alignment process? Please contact us for information about one-to-one coaching sessions to guide you along the way. We'll also be running online workshops to help people with our 8-step process.

You can contact Brad here: brad.borkan.author@gmail.com
You can contact Holly here: http://hollyworton.com/coaching

Brad Borkan

Do you want an inspiring speaker for your organization or event?

Brad is a passionate speaker with the interest and experience to show how people and businesses can make better decisions. His presentations focus on leadership, teamwork and winning against the odds – often when the odds are stacked impossibly high against success.

Topics include (but are not limited to):

- Improving your Decision Making Skills

- Lessons from Scott, Shackleton and other early
  Antarctic Explorers
- Confronting adversity
- Building effective teams
- Succeeding against all odds
- Creating organizational and team resilience

His presentations are illustrated with fascinating historical photographs from the actual expeditions. You will learn powerful techniques to improve decision making, at a personal, team or business level.

For more information on his presentations, please contact brad.borkan.author@gmail.com.

Holly Worton

Holly trained as a coach back in 2011, and she's been using her coaching skills in a variety of ways ever since then.

Her work with clients often involves a unique blend of practical coaching and two techniques—PSYCH-K® and HEW®—which work to quickly, easily, and painlessly transform beliefs at a deep level. Her zone of genius is combining these skills to help people get clear on what their big life or business vision is, and then get to the root of what's holding them back from achieving it. One thing she hears most often from clients is that taking inspired action is so much easier after working with her.

If you're curious about how to apply the techniques from this book in your own life, or if you're struggling to get from where you are to where you want to be, coaching can help.

Learn more here: http://hollyworton.com/coaching.

ABOUT THE AUTHORS

About Brad Borkan

Brad Borkan is thrilled to have collaborated on this book with Holly Worton. It has long been his passion to write a self-help book.

Brad Borkan has had a life-long interest in how people make decisions in extreme circumstances. Brad is the co-author (with David Hirzel) of two award-winning books on this topic. *When Your Life Depends on It* focuses on the life-and-death decisions made by the early Antarctic explorers. (This book reached as high as #19 on the Top 100 Best Decision Making Books of All Time.) His second book, *Audacious Goals, Remarkable Results* is a comparative history of three great people: Isambard Kingdom Brunel, Theodore Roosevelt and Roald Amundsen.

Brad has traveled to all seven continents. Originally from the US and now based in London, Brad is a former senior director at Oracle and SAP. He is an author and lecturer and has presented at business and Antarctic conferences, appeared on cable TV in the US, and has been a guest on numerous podcasts. His talks focus on leadership, teamwork and winning against the odds.

He is a Fellow of the Royal Geographical Society and a member of the Society of Authors. He has also been a contributing writer for the *Crisis Response Journal* and *Strate-*

gy+Business Magazine. To learn more or to contact Brad, please visit https://www.extreme-decisions.com/.

Facebook: https://www.facebook.com/extremedecisions/
LinkedIn: http://www.linkedin.com/in/bradborkan
Instagram: https://www.instagram.com/extremedecisions/
Twitter: https://twitter.com/PolarDecisions

––––––

About Holly Worton

Holly Worton is an author, podcaster, and publishing strategist. This is her first book collaboration, and she's thoroughly enjoyed the process of having a co-author to develop these concepts with.

Holly enjoys spending time outdoors, walking and running long-distance trails, and exploring Britain's sacred sites. Spending time in Nature is something that she finds to be deeply nourishing—it brings her a sense of expansive joy.

Her podcast and blog are about personal growth through outdoor adventures and travel. They're about our journey into the woods of ourselves: getting to know who we are, where we are, and where we're going in life so that we can create the life we want to live. They're about deepening your connection with yourself, taking inspired action, and really trusting yourself and your intuition.

She's originally from California and now lives in England, but has also lived in Spain, Costa Rica, Mexico, Chile, and Argentina. Holly is a member of the Druid order OBOD. To learn more, visit her website at www.hollyworton.com.

Podcast

You can find her podcast on Apple Podcasts, or wherever you listen to podcasts. Links to subscribe, as well as the full list of episodes, can be found here: http://www.hollyworton.com/podcast/.

Newsletter

You can stay in touch by subscribing to her newsletter on her main website: http://www.hollyworton.com/.

Goodreads: http://goodreads.com/hollyworton
Amazon.com: http://amazon.com/author/hollyworton
Instagram: https://instagram.com/hollyworton/
Facebook: https://www.facebook.com/hollywortonpage
Twitter: http://twitter.com/hollyworton
Pinterest: http://pinterest.com/hollyworton

BOOKS BY BRAD BORKAN AND HOLLY WORTON

BOOKS BY BRAD BORKAN

- When Your Life Depends on It: *Extreme Decision Making Lessons from the Antarctic*
- Audacious Goals, Remarkable Results: *How an Explorer, an Engineer and a Statesman Shaped our Modern World*
- From Hollywood to the Moon: *The Amazing Power of Very Small Teams*

BOOKS BY HOLLY WORTON

Personal growth

- The Year You Want: *Imagine Your Best Life and Design Your Ideal Year, So You Don't Leave Your Life to Chance*

Into the Woods Short Reads

- How to Add More Adventure to Your Life
- How to Develop Your Own Inner Compass: *Learn to Trust Yourself and Easily Make the Best Decisions*
- How to Practice Self Care: *Even When You Think You're Too Busy*

- How to Practice Self-Love: *Actual Steps You Can Take To Love Yourself More*
- Into the Woods Short Reads: *Box Set Books 1-5*

Business Mindset series

- Business Beliefs: *Upgrade Your Mindset to Overcome Self Sabotage, Achieve Your Goals, and Transform Your Business (and Life)*
- Business Beliefs: *A Companion Workbook*
- Business Blocks: *Transform Your Self-Sabotaging Mind Gremlins, Awaken Your Inner Mentor, and Allow Your Business Brilliance to Shine*
- Business Blocks: *A Companion Workbook*
- Business Intuition: *Tools to Help You Trust Your Own Instincts, Connect with Your Inner Compass, and Easily Make the Right Decisions*
- Business Intuition: *A Companion Workbook*
- Business Visibility: *Mindset Shifts to Help You Stop Playing Small, Dimming Your Light and Devaluing Your Magic*
- Business Visibility: *A Companion Workbook*
- Business Mindset Books: *Box Set Books 1-4*

Nature books

- If Trees Could Talk: *Life Lessons from the Wisdom of the Woods*
- If Trees Could Talk: *Life Lessons from the Wisdom of the Woods — A Companion Workbook*
- Secrets of Plant Spirit Healing With Mugwort: *Release Blockages, Get Into Alignment, and Open Up to Flow*

Walking books

- Alone on the Ridgeway: *A Tale of Two Journeys Between Avebury and Ivinghoe Beacon*
- Alone on the South Downs Way: *A Tale of Two Journeys from Winchester to Eastbourne*
- Walking the Downs Link: *Planning Guide & Reflections on Walking from St. Martha's Hill to Shoreham-by-Sea*
- Walking the Wey-South Path: *Planning Guide & Reflections on Walking from Guildford to Amberley*

En español

- Si los árboles hablaran: *enseñanzas de vida desde la sabiduría de los árboles*
- El año que quieres: *imagina la vida que deseas y planea tu año ideal, para no dejarlos al azar*

OPENING CHAPTER FROM WHEN YOUR LIFE DEPENDS ON IT

BY BRAD BORKAN AND DAVID HIRZEL

Awards

- First Place: Chanticleer International Book Awards for Insightful Non-fiction
- Winner: Wishing Shelf Awards: Best Audiobook
- Reached #19 on Top 100 Best Decision Making Books of All Time
- Finalist: Voice Arts Awards: Best Audiobook— History category.

Endorsements

"A remarkable book" *Sir Ranulph Fiennes, world's greatest living polar explorer*

"Polar book of the year" *Jonathan Shackleton, Antarctic historian*

It's Your Call

Antarctica—the early 1900's. The only communication is as far as you can shout.

You and your two companions are nearing the end of a fifteen-hundred-mile trek to a nameless spot on the South Polar Plateau.

To say conditions are harsh would be an understatement. Temperatures can get so low that you risk frostbite even when bundled in your reindeer-hide sleeping bags. The jagged, frozen landscape provides constant challenges, including the danger of crevasses cracking open unexpectedly beneath your feet, plunging you into their depths. At times you have been on the verge of starvation.

Your presence here today is the result of countless decisions great and small made along the way. Right now you are faced with a decision greater than any that came before. One of your companions has fallen so ill with scurvy he can no longer walk.

Seventy miles of dangerous terrain lie ahead before you reach the safety of your base camp, and you will have to drag him on the sledge, adding an almost unbearable weight to that of your ice-encrusted tent and the last remnants of food keeping you alive.

The reality of the situation is grim. You must maintain a steady pace each day, regardless of the weather, to reach the next depot of supplies before those on hand run out. Your daily distances have fallen off, and continue to fall. The sick man, already perilously near death, is unlikely to survive the remainder of the journey.

With his extra weight further reducing your daily mileage, neither will you and your other companion. You all know the fate that lies ahead. The sick man tells the two of you to leave him here on the Barrier and march on ahead with the sledge and supplies, to save yourselves while you can. The three of you have developed a close camaraderie during your long walk; leaving him to perish on the ice is inconceivable. The obvious, ethical, human decision: to shoulder your burden and do your best.

The situation is not so straightforward. You are seamen and the sick man is your commanding officer. He has *commanded* you to leave him behind. The one thing that has been repeatedly drilled into you throughout your entire working life is this: there is *no* occasion on which you can refuse to comply with the order of an officer.

To obey means the two of you have at least a chance at survival; to refuse is mutiny, and certain death for all three of you.

The choice is now yours—it's your call. How will you decide?

———

This was a real event faced by real people. They did have to make this call. Their decision and the outcome may surprise you ...

You will find the rest of the story in *When Your Life Depends on It: Extreme Decision Making Lessons from the Antarctic* by Brad Borkan and David Hirzel. It is available on Amazon and other online booksellers. The audiobook is available on Audible, iTunes, Spotify and all other audiobook sites.

INTRODUCTION FROM THE YEAR YOU WANT

BY HOLLY WORTON

For the first 35 years of my life, I just let things happen to me. I didn't set goals, I didn't really make plans. Life just happened.

And it wasn't always great. In fact, I got myself into some bad situations in life. I had a really dark and difficult decade that was tough to get through.

Then I learned how to be intentional about creating the life I wanted to live. I learned how to plan the year that I wanted to experience. And I created a simple process for making it happen.

I have an intensive annual planning system that I go through every year. I spend time looking over how I experienced the current year, and what I want to do differently in the new year. I create a clear list of goals, plans, and projects, and I review them on a regular basis throughout the year to make sure I stay on track.

This planning system is how I create the life that I want to live.

It's also how I achieved the following in 2020 (at the time of publication):

- Wrote 32 blog posts
- Produced 40 podcast episodes
- Published 13 books
- Appeared on national TV in the UK on ITV's This Morning
- Appeared as a guest on 5 podcasts
- Walked 150 miles around Wiltshire and Sussex on my March trip
- Walked 87+ miles on the Ridgeway National Trail
- Completed my Wildlife Tracking and Identification course
- Achieved my Advanced Bushcraft award

However, there's something important thing for me to point out: to me, life is not about racking up achievements. It's about creating the life that I want to live and having the experiences that I want. I love writing and creating, and I love appearing on TV and podcasts to talk about my books. I also love nature, so outdoor adventures and courses are important to me. All of these things give me the feeling of expansive joy that I seek in life.

And this is what I want for you.

Now, for the first time, I'm sharing my system. I'm super excited to be able to walk you through my process, so you can create the life that you want to live—year by year.

I believe that by consciously planning our lives, we can course-correct each year and create our ideal life full of happiness and joy.

For me, it didn't happen from one day to the next, or even from one year to the next.

It's still a work in progress. But each year is exponentially better than the year before—and it's all thanks to my planning process.

I'm going to keep this introduction simple, so you can dig right in and get started.

———

The Year You Want is a personal journal that helps you to imagine your best life and design your ideal year, so you don't leave life to chance.

There are two parts to the workbook:

1. First, we evaluate the year that's just passed, so we can see what went right—and what could be improved and also what we can let go of that isn't serving us to make space for new experiences and adventures.
2. Second, we plan all the details of what we want to experience in the new year. We plan projects, set goals, and create a plan to achieve them.

Are you ready to stop simply existing and instead start living a fulfilling life that's full of joy and adventures?

You can begin *The Year You Want* at any time of the year.

You'll simply adjust it to evaluate the previous 12 months of your life, and then plan the next 12 months—whether that's in December, March, July, or September. The sooner you start, the sooner you'll be living your dream and inspired life.

It's available as a paperback on Amazon and other online booksellers.